May 15, 1999

F

For Terie,
Keep hold of the dream! Someday
you will have the sanctuary garden
of your dreams and it will be
beau-ti full.

Peace be with you,

Tracy
Saint
99

Christopher Forrest McDowell

Tricia Clark-McDowell

Line illustrations by Tricia Clark-McDowell
Watercolors by Hanna Yoshimura

A FIRESIDE BOOK
Published by Simon & Schuster

The Sanctuary Garden

Creating a Place of Refuge
in Your Yard
or Garden

FIRESIDE
Rockefeller Center
1230 Avenue of the Americas
New York, NY 10020

Designed by Katy Riegel
Manufactured in the United States of America

1   3   5   7   9   10   8   6   4   2
Library of Congress Cataloging-in-Publication Data
McDowell, Christopher Forrest, 1948–
The sanctuary garden : creating a place of refuge in your yard or garden / [Christopher Forrest McDowell,
Tricia Clark-McDowell; line illustrations by Tricia Clark-McDowell; watercolors
by Hanna Yoshimura].
        p.   cm.
"A Fireside book."
Includes bibliographical references.
1. Sanctuary gardens.   I. Clark-McDowell, Tricia, 1950–   II. Title.
SB454.3.S25M34   1998
712—dc21   98-12770
                                                                CIP

ISBN 0-684-84637-3

To all those who are willing

to envision and create sanctuary

within this greater sanctuary

called Earth

Acknowledgements

Sincere gratitude to all our dear friends and family, who over the years planted seeds of love and support—thank you for your faith in us. We are especially thankful for those who have inspired us with their gardens, their stories, and their dreams for a better world—we honor your vision.

We honor those people and organizations who tirelessly work to create sanctuary in this world of need. We are especially moved by the efforts of Self-Realization Fellowship, the Earthstewards Network, and SEVA.

Thank you Jenny Bent, our agent, who discovered us by following her own heart. And to our editor at Simon & Schuster, Laurie Chittenden, whose sensitivity and intuition shaped this book's content. We are grateful that you believed in us enough to come and experience Cortesia Sanctuary for yourself. And to the art department and all those at Simon & Schuster involved in the design and publicity of this book—thank you for believing in our dream.

Our deepest, heartfelt thanks to our friend and artist, Hanna Yoshimura. For several years now you have chronicled Cortesia Sanctuary's blossoming through your artistic gifts. We are also sincerely indebted to you, Harriet Kofalk, even as you now rest in the Sanctuary of Heaven—your gift of the Seed of Peace is forever planted in our heart's work. And to you, Sonji, our dear daughter—thank you for patiently understanding why the words *garden* and *sanctuary* keep popping up dozens of times a day in family conversation. It is our intent to leave a legacy of hope for all future children.

Finally, to those of you who still wonder what your true livelihood might be, may we suggest: Acknowledge your own sacred power and unique gifts. Do something filled with heart and a great amount of love that will not harm a soul. Do it for this Earth, do it for that divine presence that lives within each and every being and touchstone of Nature. Do this work the best you can, stand back from it now and then, and watch it gracefully collapse into place.

Contents

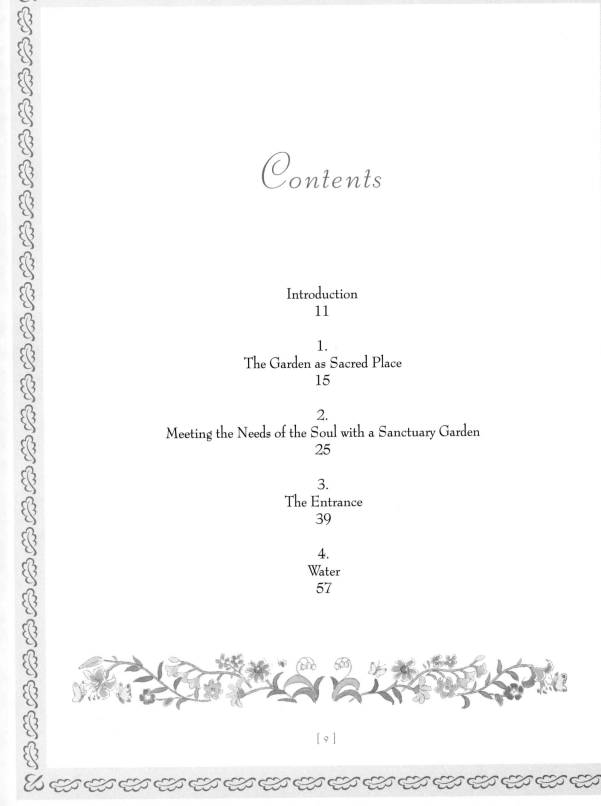

Contents

Introduction

My earliest recollection of the feeling of sanctuary, as I would now describe it, came when I was a girl of six or seven. Standing in our backyard in a quarter-acre bed of lilies-of-the-valley, my nose buried in the fragrant bouquet held lovingly in my hands, I was in heaven. My family (I was one of eight children) picked and sold these lovely flowers every spring around Mother's Day. This paid for our family vacation in the summer to a rustic cabin high in the Colorado Rockies. Climbing those grand mountains over the years—every one that we could see from our cabin—developed the strength of my character, laying latent within me, and kindled my deep love of Nature.

I still grow lilies-of-the-valley and climb mountains, though I now live thousands of miles from my childhood home. And I carry in me the flowering of those soulful seeds planted so long ago. Within each of us, noble seeds have been sown, somewhere, sometime. They silently grow over the years, stimulating us to manifest our deepest desires. Can we remember? More important, are we watering them and nurturing them day by day in the deep, rich tilth of our soul's yearning for fulfillment?

Over and over again, I return to the roots of my childhood, striving to recreate that original pure being within the contemporary vision of my life. It is in the solitude and safety of my Sanctuary Garden that I have experienced the deepest sense of peace. Peace with my past, acceptance of the long years of loneliness I endured, and forgiveness of those who have hurt me perhaps without ever knowing. Because of my Sanctuary Garden I have also learned to forgive my own failures. Nature is a most patient teacher.

My first garden was planted in 1974, to salve the heartache of my dearest friend and lover's death. With that and each succeeding garden, I learned to weave my story, however tragic or flawed, into the seasonal familiarity of Nature's cycles. Many have reverently tilled the soil before me. Many will do so after I am gone. But we all have the potential to share one thing—the sense of sanctuary and solace through our connection to Nature.

Perhaps you have developed an interior sense of sanctuary but it still lies hidden within you; let it emerge into the light of day. Let it come to full and beautiful expression in a physical form. When Forrest, my husband, came into my life some 18 years ago, that is when I finally began to allow the inner to become the outer, the little girl to speak through the woman, the real garden to manifest. Now I am ready to share this journey and my voice with you, in that hope that it might inspire you in some small way to believe in your own voice.

I have great appreciation for Tricia's journey toward sanctuary and into my life. I remember my first Sanctuary Garden. As a young boy, I could say it was my backyard where King Imagination ruled, but it was more than that. There was a certain place in the yard that gave me comfort for many years. It was the shade of a birch tree under which I sat. I came to this tree to escape my father's wrath and abuse, to write poetry, to pray, and to think. I came here to ponder love and to celebrate its anticipation, fantasy, or memory. I came here to play and compose music, to write songs and ballads. I came here to watch Nature and to feel my breath. Above all, however, I came to sit beneath this birch for peace. As I matured, the birch itself grew and stretched out its canopy into an ever-widening umbrella of shade. My sanctuary began to fill the yard, just as my need to help others with their ills and concerns expanded with each passing year. When I left my parent's nest, the seed of sanctuary went with me. The birch's gift of peace followed me into mountains and beside rivers and sat within me in meditation on ocean shores and amongst wildflower meadows. Still, not until I met Tricia did my sanctuary return to a garden, which seems a proper place to nurture a profound spiritual relationship with another human, Nature, and God.

We drew in our awe in one simultaneous breath: "Oh, my God, this is it!" Thus was our first sight of the twenty-two acres of land we now call Cortesia. The house sits in the clearing of an intimate meadow with towering 100-year-old firs all around. A Hansel and Gretel house with lots of windows and no storage space. The garden is tucked into the corner of a larger meadow to the west. Today, its two acres flows from the woodland shade near the house to the open sun of the tree-lined meadow. Twelve years ago, you would have had to bushwack to reach the tiny garden long forgotten by the previous owner. This forlorn spot of Nature was the one intriguing paradox about the man who had stewarded this property so well. How could he have appreciated the house and forest only to leave the garden in waste?

Now, another new family was going to take over the land. We had left a small university neighborhood house whose whimsical charm was only exceeded by what you might call an *interesting* garden. That garden, in the formulative years of our relationship, mirrored the very state of our chaotic partnership. It grew every which way alongside the driveway, for all passersby to witness. Little did anyone know that our first garden together was an epiphany to our triumphs and struggles as a couple.

Actually, the garden's value was mostly in the green and leafy retreat it provided each of us from our marriage. This is where that old seed of sanctuary, held within the unique journeys of our separate lives, was to be planted. The survival of the garden, in a sense, came to symbolize the survival of our relationship. So, it was the *feeling* of sanctuary within the garden that gave us the greatest pleasure—for it was a special place to lose oneself, a safe place to think, contemplate, create, heal, and comfort the soul. At that moment, we were not fully aware of the power of a garden to create sanctuary for its visitors and keepers.

We came to Cortesia because we wanted to place roots deep into the Earth. We wanted our newborn daughter to experience the Earth as her mother, too. We also wanted sanctuary from the city, from the incessant drone of machines and human babble, yet we wanted to know that culture was nearby. We wanted to love the woods and the soil, and we desired to include Nature in our marriage. This is why our first act, in the late fall of our arrival, was to plant just one little plot in the withered garden as a statement of communion, of surrender to this Creation.

The garden has long been a metaphor for life. Its roots are anchored in Paradise—a sacred place where body and soul can dwell in grace. The garden has also mirrored our human play and celebration of Nature. By enclosing a small portion of this Earth in a garden, we have created an unwritten covenant with the Divine: that we will respect, honor, and enhance that which Nature has to offer.

Beyond its practical aspects, gardening—be it of the soil or soul—can lead us on a philosophical and spiritual exploration that is nothing less than a journey into the depths of our own sacredness and the sacredness of all beings. After all, there *must* be something more mystical beyond the garden gate, something that satisfies the soul's attraction to beauty, peace, solace, and celebration. To begin exploration of sanctuary is to create a link to the Divine. We humans are only one of the keepers of our garden, of this Earth, of our relationship to spirit. Our duty is to nurture peace, beauty, harmony, gratitude, compassion, and reverence—within our lives, within our gardens. We are all gardeners, each capable of keeping a Sanctuary Garden.

As author Thomas Moore suggests in *The Re-enchantment of Everyday Life:* "There is an enchantment that arises out of the garden spirit, which, for all the variety of gardens around the world, is unique." As longtime gardeners and devotees of meditation, we are certain of the existence of a Garden Spirit. Therefore, be it matters of the garden or matters of the soul, we should each be driven by the purity of our intentions to create a special place for ourselves in the world. Where is your Sanctuary Garden?

The Sanctuary Garden is both a new form of garden design and a whole-life philosophy. Its seven design elements not only provide a structure by which to create and practice your own garden design, but also suggest a way to embrace the sacredness of life.

The key to achieving sanctuary is to honor and celebrate our broader human relationship with Nature and Spirit, not just plants. Most gardeners will say that gardening is primarily about plants—which ones to select, grow, propagate, and nurture. As you will discover in this book, the seven design elements of a Sanctuary Garden speak less about vegatation than they do about other, often overlooked considerations:

- *Creating a special entrance* that enfolds and invites the visitor into sanctuary.
- *Effectively using water* for its psychological, spiritual, and physical effects.
- *Creatively using color* and lighting (be it from plants or natural/human-designed lighting sources) to elicit emotion, comfort, or awe in the visitor.
- *Designing sitting areas* that enfold the visitor into the sanctuary experience.
- *Highlighting natural features as anchor points,* including the use of rocks, wood, natural fences, screens, trellises, wind, sound, and so on.
- *Integrating art* that enhances the overall mood.
- *Providing habitat and features* to attract a diversity of wildlife.

The form a Sanctuary Garden takes is not as important as the marriage of intention between the garden's Keeper and Nature. It is less important to use all seven design elements than it is to pick one or two and elevate their presence in your garden with sincerity and creativity. A lone bench beneath an arbor of passionflowers or grapes, for example, succeeds as a perfect Sanctuary Garden, just as much as an intricately designed landscape. The Keeper's sincerity should be directed toward honoring any of the design elements: a plant is well-selected, a bench is in the right spot; an outcropping of rock is showcased; color, lighting, and texture enhance the drama; and certain pieces of art seem to be a natural part of the landscape, almost as if they come out of the Earth themselves.

To be sure, part of the attraction of a Sanctuary Garden is that it reflects the unique insight of its Keeper. There are many ways to comfort the soul, and throughout this book we offer practical wisdom from our own experience as well as from the many people we have met over the years who have followed this philosophy in their own lives and gardens with success. We know, for example, that some paths embrace more diversity of wildlife and vegetation, more friendships, and support in life. Others are quite content with a smaller space or level of simplicity. While still others embrace spontaneity. Indeed, the Sanctuary Garden is a place and opportunity to comfort the many dimensions of the soul. Much like Nature, the soul is whimsical and spontaneous, moody and vulnerable—one day melancholy, another day exhuberant, and yet another day contemplative. In the Sanctuary Garden, all sincere expressions are honored. For this reason, and far from being perfect or contrived, every Sanctuary Garden is a unique, special, and sacred place for the soul to dwell in.

1

The Garden as Sacred Place

We may have to learn again the mystery of the garden:

how its external characteristics model the heart itself,

and how the soul is a garden enclosed, our own

perpetual paradise where we can

be refreshed and restored.

—THOMAS MOORE,

The Re-enchantment of Everyday Life

There is a theology to gardening that few of us consider, but to understand this theology means relinquishing much control—our arsenal of books, techniques, tools, chemicals, fertilizers, fancy hybrids, and expectations. Yet, that is exactly what we must do if we are to fully embrace a more spiritual form of gardening. As a part of Nature we must learn to enter our garden as if it were truly sacred, we must learn to enter with humility.

The garden itself is not fully Nature, for Nature is much more untamed and powerful. Nature is for the most part indifferent to our human will, and a garden's walls are just not high enough to keep out the will of Nature.

I have seen Nature fly over our garden fence as a seed to unexpectedly plant itself next to the maple tree. Each spring I notice when She journeys from another part of the Earth as a swallow to nest within the fir next to my writing studio. Her rain crosses oceans, mountains, and plains to pour mineral-rich nourishment into the soil. As a mole, She burrows beneath the gate from the adjacent field, to make a summer home by the strawberries. And, late in the day, I have seen Her cast an orange sunset glow from the horizon onto the wisteria arbor. These faces of Nature do not depend upon a garden to conduct their daily or seasonal ritual, nor do they acknowledge human boundaries.

As gardeners, however, we *do* enclose Nature. And we *do* call it our garden, but in so doing how many of us realize the opportunity we have to create an extraordinary partnership between ourselves and the Earth?

One of the most powerful examples of our relationship to the land came to me when witnessing the end of the war in Bosnia. I was touched to learn that the first act of many of the citizens of Sarajevo after the war was to till and plant their gardens. This in itself was a brave gesture, one full of trust that, after many previously short-lived truces, the war could now truly be called over. Imagine the

Three Devotions of a Reverential Way of Life

THE DEVOTION TO *Peace*

Peace is probably the final frontier that our soul seeks. It has been said that we must alter our lives in order to alter our hearts, for it is impossible to live one way and pray another. Indeed, it is this peace within our heart that can unlock the deep abiding relationship possible with all other beings on Earth. You can understand, therefore, that your devotion to peace is reinforced by your commitment to finding sanctuary everyday. You can find peace within sanctuary and you can carry that peace with you in your worldly activities.

THE DEVOTION TO *Place*

A sense of place is a deep dignifying component of life. Every human, animal, plant, structure, or object is enriched by having a significant relationship to place. You are

---

value of that little plot of Nature in each householder's life, and the sense of safety they must have felt despite recent horrors. Elevated to a critical symbol of survival for body and spirit, we could even say the garden was a sacred place worth fighting for. To be sure, the gardens of the citizens of Sarajevo signified hope, security, peace. And, in this sense, each garden was a sanctuary.

When Tricia and I began gardening we were, in a way, reclaiming a spiritual relationship with the Earth. It is not by accident that about the time we began our efforts we were deeply affected by the philosophy of Saint Francis. Francis's *Canticle for Brother Sun and Sister Moon* reflected our love and passion for Nature and God, but it was the ancient French word, *cortese,* that best exemplified our intentions. *Cortese* literally means manners, or specifically the behavior and etiquette expected of one who serves at a noble court. The most obvious English translation is "courtesy," but courtesy today has a more superficial meaning than it did long ago. The original use of the word *cortese* was to describe nobility of character and conduct, that is, the recognition of rights, duties, gifts, and privileges as they exist in a reciprocal relationship.

Standing amidst our garden, the breath of long-forgotten spirits calling out through the surrounding towering firs, Tricia and I were transported to a whole other way of living on Earth. Not just in our garden, we discovered, but in our marriage, family, friendships, service to others, and our relationship to the Divine. Each day became a journey into the garden of our soul, and this

already aware of this, to be sure. However, deepen your understanding of place through the eyes of sanctuary. Sanctuary *is* about place. This is why a special setting in your yard and garden or a nearby park or the mountains can be a sanctuary. It is certainly not out of the question that even a small area is a place worthy of sanctuary. Truly, a value of sanctuary is that it gets us in touch with places that have meaning to us— where we can be more ourselves than any other place—places that feel sacred.

THE DEVOTION TO *Stewardship*

Stewardship is the right action necesssary to live peacefully in the world in whatever place we might find ourselves. *Stewardship* means "keeper of the place." Therefore, stewardship is about relationship with whomever or whatever. Sanctuary elevates our awareness of the right types of behaviors and activities necessary to maintain honoring and peaceful relationships with all the beings and objects we come in contact with. In sanctuary, we practice reverence and courtesy—noble behaviors that we can take back into our worldly activities and relationships.

Cortesian philosophy reacquainted us with an old philosophy of oneness with all of life on Earth. It is quite significant that the first ornament we brought to our land was a statue of St. Francis, where to this day in our meadow it has weathered the many seasons of our actions and the rhythmic flow of Nature.

Clearly, the creation of a Sanctuary Garden is just one step toward honoring a different vision of the world. A Cortesian philosophy, expressed through the concept of sanctuary, reconnects us with something very soulful about life on Earth. It asks us to consciously consider establishing a covenant that helps to answer this key question: "How can I live on Earth today so that my life and all other life is served well?"

We believe the answer to this question lies in embracing love and goodwill. Love in its Earthly manifest form must surely be the Nature which enfolds our total beingness both inwardly and outwardly. Love is the garden we grow in and the garden that grows within our soul. If we forget Nature, we forget how to love, and in forgetting how to love, we forget how to garden.

THE SANCTUARY GARDEN
AS A SACRED STORY

The story of gardening is not too different from that of sanctuary. Almost every culture on Earth has a creation myth that embodies a paradise or safe haven. Many cultures describe this paradise in terms of a garden wherein dwells peace and harmony among all creatures and vegetation. In fact, the word *paradise* comes from the 2400 year old Persian word *pairi-daeza,* meaning "beautiful fenced-in garden."

Theologian Matthew Fox speaks of the "original blessing" of creation, as it is characterized in the mythical Garden of Eden. Part of the mystique of this blessing of creation is the idea of sacred enclosure, suggesting the safety of a Divine Matrix. This sense of sacred containment is just as valid when describing our garden as it is in describing our human body, planet Earth, or even the form of a tree, rock, or animal. Each form of life, therefore, can be seen as a type of sanctuary, a haven into which the energy of Nature and God is poured as an act of love.

When you create a garden with deep intent, you are creating a sacred place in which, like the Divine, you can pour out your love, creativity and compassion. You are, in a sense, creating a small sanctuary in which your soul and the soul of the world may dwell. This sanctuary garden becomes your own creation story to nurture within the body of this Earth—your form of Eden. And, as this paradise grows outside, so it grows as well within your heart.

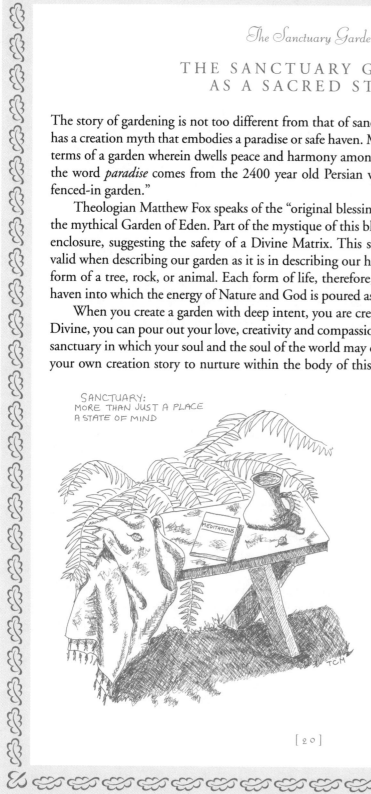

SANCTUARY:
MORE THAN JUST A PLACE
A STATE OF MIND

In many respects, sanctuary cannot be defined adequately in plain physical terms, for it resides both within the soul and in the world. We find it sometimes as grace during the day—a special place or relationship that comforts us, regenerates our spirit, and deepens our connection to life. But we also find sanctuary outside of time and place. In sanctuary we can re-experience a natural religion removed from human dogma, conflict, or argument. Benches become pews, trees become preachers, and the choir of flowers sing in great joy to the wind's organ voice. Mountain gardens—those intimate and expansive wildflower meadows, boulder-strewn amphitheaters, brooks, and lakeside waysides—are ancient sanctuaries. But even in our backyard we can hear and witness God naturally outside our backdoor—between our toes, warm on our skin, abuzz.

If you create a Sanctuary Garden in your life, remember why you are doing so. It has something to do with nurturing peace within and without, with fostering a relationship in a special place, even if it is simply a chair sitting on your porch or balcony with a few potted plants. Let that be your Sanctuary Garden. The purity of your devotion and intention is what matters, and not what other people think. When you practice reverence for life, nonjudgement, and compassion, you are giving of yourself to bring more joy, beauty, hope, and peace into the world. By embracing your sacredness you are pre-

IN THE SHRINE-
TIBETAN PRAYER FLAGS
& WINDCHIMES HANG
AMONGST THE KIWI VINES

pared to embrace the sacredness of the world. Do these things and you become the Keeper of your garden, and the Keeper of your soul.

The beginning, for each of us, of our spiritual reconstruction is a reverential treatment of life. Reverence, in and of itself, emerges as a deeper understanding of the ecology of place, of Earth, and of ourselves. It is not only a principle of *understanding and receiving* the beauty of the world. It is a principle of appropriate *behavior*. Reverence for life means re-enchantment with the world and celebration of the miracle of its creation.

THE SANCTUARY GARDEN
AS A SACRED HEARTH

The concept of the hearth is sorely missing in modern culture, commonly replaced by the blue glow of television and its mute observers. Although the idea of a hearth is often attached to a fireplace, it is probably the *feeling* a hearth evokes that gives it great value. The hearth is a place where interaction, communication, and sharing is alive: the telling of stories, the teaching and construction of handicrafts between generations, the sense of communion and safety. It is a sacred place where the feeling of family, home, land, friends, thoughts, and God renews hope.

Hearth is a powerful symbol. Now, imagine a place where beings, species, vegetation, and natural elements such as water, wind, light, and sound are honored. Your Sanctuary Garden, whether you realize it or not, is like a home, and can become a welcome hearth.

In this one word—*hearth*—we see several words that remind us of a more noble way of living and being of service on Earth. First, there is the very word *earth,* to remind us that this Earth and the soil out of which everything seems to grow is a sanctuary itself worthy of honoring. We also see in hearth the words *ear* and *hear,* to remind us of our human duty as Keepers to listen and be aware of the needs of all beings, species, and spirits. The word *art* is also there to remind us of that which seizes and arrests our soul—the artistry, craft, beauty, and thrift that is Nature and the creative expression of humans. And finally, there is *heart,* as in *heartfelt.* It is truly the feeling and thinking heart that can remind and lead us continuously to a higher self that is hopeful, reverent, gracious, humble, honoring, courteous, and respectful.

When you ponder the creation of your Sanctuary Garden, you are setting in motion spiritual energy. This is the natural outcome of defining a boundary or location with reverent intent, and creating what the ancient Greeks called *temenos,* or "sacred enclosure." Like a hearth or shrine, it becomes empowered by repeated visits, by good deeds, by the desire to honor the nature of spirit and the spirit of Nature in their most simple or complex forms.

Your garden, therefore, as simple or complex as you desire it to be, contains a spirit reflective of the marriage between human and Nature. Created as a sanctuary, it is a safe haven between you, the Earth, and the Divine. It is of Nature. It is of Spirit. It is of body and soul that creates a spiritual bond between human and Nature.

We have found that one of the first and most important gestures in establishing a Sanctuary Garden is defining its place and honoring it with a name. The simplicity or extravagance of a garden is not important in its naming, although the mere mention of the White Garden at Sissinghurst Castle in England conjures up images of one of the most revered and imitated gardens in the world. Let your garden's name represent your fondness for Nature. Consider having a sign made with your garden's name on it to hang near the entrance.

We named our sanctuary and gardens *Cortesia* to reflect our reverence for life. After you give

Naming Your Sanctuary

Christening a special place with a name, just like a person, is both an act of honor and celebration. Our sanctuary, Cortesia Sanctuary, was created on Thanksgiving Day. A number of friends were invited and an evening candlelight procession with chanting and drumming was made to the entrance. Here we formed a circle, said a prayer, named our setting, and hung a sign. Cortesia now *feels* not only special but sacred. Here are some tips for naming your setting:

· Sit and spend some quiet meditation time in your setting. Feel its energy and uniqueness. Let a name just come to you.
· Does the name feel right to you? Let a day or two go by. As you enter your sanctuary, think of it now by name. If you like it, then that's the name it wants to have.
· Create a special ritual to christen your setting.
· Consider having a special sign made with your sanctuary's name.
· Keep a journal and photo album of life in your sanctuary over the years.
· Consider joining other like-minded people who have created and registered their setting as a sanctuary. There are many around the world—information is provided on page 184

your garden a name, we encourage you to create a ceremony that gives birth to its setting. You may even wish to create a journal in your sanctuary's name, and to chronicle the history of your relationship to it. On a stormy winter day, your garden stories can make wonderful reading by the warmth of a fire, and they can serve to rekindle fond memories.

2

Meeting the Needs of the Soul with a Sanctuary Garden

Don't go outside your house to see flowers.

My friend, don't bother with that excursion.

Inside your body there are flowers.

One flower has a thousand petals.

That will do for a place to sit.

Sitting there you will have a glimpse of beauty

inside the body and out of it,

before gardens and after gardens.

—ROBERT BLY, *The Kabir Book*

How does a garden give sanctuary to the soul?

We know that when we are feeling down, wounded, or are simply world-weary, we need solace. Perhaps we feel melancholy or, conversely, full of childlike exuberance—here, too, we sometimes need a place to express ourselves and simply be one with our spirit. We can't always be preoccupied with the needs of our body, our daily duties and obligations, or the needs of others such as family, friends, or employer. Our worldly activities, whether we realize it or not, must find balance with the sacred or spiritual. Pure and simple, this much-needed balance is an issue of survival for our soul!

In the last chapter we shared how the garden is our opportunity as humans to acknowledge and embrace the spirit of Nature and the nature of Spirit. Over the years, we have begun to articulate just what it is that our soul needs, and how the sacred place of a Sanctuary Garden can begin to meet those needs. I want to share some of our discoveries with you. Perhaps then you will be better prepared to see the potential for your own Sanctuary Garden to evolve using the design elements shared in this book.

THE NEED FOR SACRED TIME & SPACE

A special setting, and especially one that we have created ourselves, always seems to give us permission to take the time and space to be in it. In a sacred space like a Sanctuary Garden, we come back into owning our time—and, thus, owning ourselves. As both wellness practitioners and gardeners, we know many people with stressful jobs who find spiritual rejuvenation in their backyards. This is their place of sanctuary they immediately visit upon returning home from work.

A "ONE PLANTER GARDEN"

For most people, sacred time and space seems difficult, if not impossible, to come by. Some relegate it to an hour or so in church on Sunday, a visit to a park or someone else's nice garden, or perhaps just a yearly vacation. In the latter instance, people may look for sacred time and space only in faraway locations like a wilderness area, national park, or an exotic place like Hawaii or Europe.

It is with good reason that people value the special time and space of vacation. The word itself comes from the Latin *vacatio,* meaning "freedom from service." Indeed, what makes time and space sacred *is* the freedom from the drone of everyday obligations, duties, and stress.

For a good part of my life I believed that taking special time and space meant going far away from home after a long build-up of frustration and stress. Gradually, however, I became aware that I needed sacred time and space every day and close at hand. My high-strung nature, like a guitar strung too tight, often reached a breaking point in my activities and relationships, until I finally began to find more effective ways to calm myself. Meditation came first, but gardening was the next instrument I discovered. Unfortunately, for a long time I applied the same level of compulsiveness to growing plants as to the rest of my daily life. In fact, gardening became an obsession.

At first, I worked very hard in my garden. It was a pursuit more intellectual and physical than spiritual. Nevertheless, beginning the process of gardening quickened my own evolution toward soulfulness. Perhaps this was inevitable. In any case, once begun, there was no turning back on the journey. I meditated, I gardened. I tilled my soul, I tilled the soil. Gradually, gardening became more like meditation. Breathe in, breathe out. My breath became the needed breath of the plants, their breath my own needed infusion for survival. Beyond time and space, both gardening and meditation became reciprocal exchanges of energy and my own cheaply fashioned wristwatch began to break down.

Actually, I have worn a watch for a total of three weeks in my life. It was given to me by an eighty-six-year-old woman at the retirement center where I worked as activity director. She hoped the watch (once her husband's) would help me to be more "time responsible." She should have known better! I wore the watch until it went through the washing machine in one of my pockets.

It never worked again. Consequently, I knew once and for all that watches were not for me.

Inspired by my own garden at home, I organized a garden club at the retirement center. I was amazed at how important this activity became to the elders. In wheelchairs and walkers they came, hobbling with canes, weakened from cancer, in recovery from heart attacks. One man was nearly blind. They each had their own poignant life story to tell, often fraught with difficulties. In the garden, it was as if they were young again, having been released from the leathery skin of age and disease. Indeed, for each participant this was very special time in a very special place. Call it sacred if you will. Sometimes, it took all the energy someone had just to water their raised bed, or to pull out a few weeds, but that didn't seem to matter. Through these simple activities their spirits were being healed, as the body and mind were drawn into a paradise beyond time and place. These elders' gardens were giving them sanctuary.

Once we have found a bit of time and a sweet place that seems so special that it seems to grow in its own accord in our heart, we are certain to return again and again with a loyalty that is fierce. Gardening, I have learned, can do this to people. It has long done that for me. You see, worldly watches can never measure the significance of the time the soul spends with Nature. We don't write this activity on the calendar—it just happens because we have surrendered to it.

Surrender to the gentle call of your Sanctuary Garden, even if it is only at this moment an idea. Cultivate and honor your vision, however simple. Gather the few tools necessary (shovel, garden fork, trowel, wheelbarrow, and pruning shears), but don't get carried away with that. Your most important tool is your heart's desire—the desire to create a place where you can be more yourself than any other place. Get yourself a little bench or stool that can easily be moved around the yard, viewing your potential sanctuary space from all angles at every time of the day and night. Let the dream articulate itself, little by little or in great bursts, however it comes.

I recently met a woman who had attended a talk I had given on creating sanctuary. A few weeks later, she came to one of our open gardens where she sat next to our little waterfall and pond for a long time. Finally, toward the end of the day, she told me she had just bought a house in town. "I am not going to plant anything in my yard for a year," she told me with assurance. "I want to better understand what is already there and get to know the spirit of the place."

I was touched by this comment. Clearly, she was willing to cultivate her connection to place, little by little, season by season, before making any changes. Sit and watch, listen and learn, in the place you envision as your Sanctuary Garden. Whenever you feel ready to dive in, do so humbly, with a beginner's mind, open heart, and an empty bowl of gratitude.

Once you begin to see the garden of your soul and the garden

Visualizing Your Sanctuary Garden

A first step in creating your sanctuary is to visualize it. Sit in a comfortable chair with a piece of paper. Write down images, thoughts, and ideas that come to mind. Think about other natural places you have been to that felt very soulful and replenishing to your spirit. Here are some ideas to inspire you:

· Imagine that your Sanctuary Garden is where you go to feel a full sense of communion with Nature and your own sense of spirit within. What feelings do you want to evoke in visiting your sanctuary?

· Imagine standing at the very entrance to your sanctuary, or looking out at it through a window. What attracts you to it and beckons you to enter, leaving your cares behind?

· Generally speaking, there are usually one or more striking features (natural or man-made) that may draw you or a visitor into your sanctuary. What would these features be?

· Do you see a sitting spot or two? Where will these be placed and what form will they take?

outside your door as a beautiful haven awaiting your reverent love and intentions, you will never be the same. You will have awakened the Spirit of Place that gives solace and comfort to all beings who enter, visit, or dwell within. And small miracles can begin to happen. One discovery leads to another and another. This is what Forrest and I call *sanctuary work,* and it may well be some of the most important work you ever do.

THE NEED FOR
RE-ENCHANTMENT

The Sanctuary Garden is a natural lure that may gently draw us into its magical web of enchantment. We become like little children in its midst, awed by Nature's exquisite artistry, which in turn is enhanced by our appreciation and thoughtful touch. Thomas Moore, in his wonderful book, *The Re-enchantment of Everyday Life,* speaks eloquently about the soul's need for enchantment:

· Imagine the sight and sound of water and how soothing it is to your spirit. What water feature exists in your imaginary sanctuary? Where will it be located and what will the lighting and plantings be like?

· Imagine there is a special "room" in your garden/yard that is an intimate setting. Visualize and describe it in full detail.

· Do you hear the sounds of Nature? What especially touches you—birds singing, the wind rustling, water moving? How are you going to incorporate Nature's symphony into your sanctuary?

· Visualize wildlife—birds, bees, butterflies, frogs, and the like—living in or visiting your sanctuary. What features (nesting boxes, feeders, baths, ponds) do you see, and where?

· Imagine the types of vegetation in your setting—trees, grasses, shrubs, vines, flowers, potted plants. What are your favorites and where are they located?

· Imagine a prominent feature or two—a special trellis, bench, circle herb garden, rock garden, pond, large boulder, dominant tree, striking fence.

· Imagine creating your porch, courtyard, or balcony as a miniature Nature sanctuary. What would it contain?

". . . To make local nature a concrete element in daily life is a necessary initial step in the re-enchantment of our individual lives . . . Enchantment is to a large extent founded in the spirituality inherent in earthly nature . . . Our task is to re-expand our very idea of spirituality to include the lowliest of things and the most particular and familiar haunts of nature."

Most of us remember periods in our childhood where clearly we were in love with whatever Nature existed around us. As a girl, I delighted in playing with earthworms, climbing trees, smelling flowers, and catching fireflies on warm summer nights. I passionately loved watering, so my father gave me the job of hand-watering all the new grass and trees he planted. Watching the rainbow-laden water spray out of the nozzle and soak into the dark earth was an experience of which I never tired. I still enjoy watering today, though in the interest of conservation I now know how to use deep watering techniques, which are outlined in many gardening books.

Anthropologist Ashley Montague once said that adults are merely diseased children. I think

Three Key Qualities of an Outdoor Sanctuary

AESTHETIC ATTRACTION

To co-create a sanctuary with Nature is a wonderful experience. Imagine you are privileged to be an artist at Nature's canvas. Try, therefore, to set a tone, evoke a feeling, enhance Nature's drama and character. Create an entrance that is inviting. The types of vegetation are important, as are their placement and color. Equally important is the use of wood, rocks, water, trellises, and the like. These, including sitting areas, wind chimes, birdbaths, and garden art are worthy artistic additions that give your outdoor sanctuary appealing ambience.

SOUL ATTRACTION

Perhaps the most magnetic quality of a sanctuary is how it affects one's spirit. This can be attributed to the way it has been created so as to honor and celebrate life. Try, therefore, to care for the three elements of earth, air, and water. Enrich and plant the soil organically. Celebrate the wind with tall wispy grasses and wind chimes. Honor water

he is right, if part of the disease is caused by a lack of Nature in our diet. I never grew out of my childhood love for Nature. However, for many adults, this precious relationship recedes far into the background and may be entirely lost for years on end. Yet, it is precisely during our adult years that we need more than ever to maintain our sense of enchantment with the world around us, in particular, the natural world.

Thomas Moore partially defines enchantment as "a state of rapture and ecstasy in which the soul comes to the foreground, and the literal concerns of survival and daily preoccupation at least momentarily fade into the background." Don't we all crave such an experience? Not just once or twice in our life or each year, but repeatedly.

Every feature of the Sanctuary Garden, however practical its design and implementation, can indeed be conceived of and viewed through the crystalline lens of enchantment. We must simply relearn what we knew as children. The Sanctuary Garden becomes our healer, in this sense. It lets the imagination have free reign over and beyond the influence of a mind filled with schedules, worries and routines. Such a garden experience allows us to see anew with awe and wonder, as peace and tranquility, reverence, and hope are planted tenderly in our heart.

with good conservation practices and water features. Appealing to the soul's need for beauty, tender a variety of flowering vegetation, and integrate garden art and crafts, the more naturally made the better. Lastly, give that contemplative part of yourself a special sitting area, bench, or chair. Set these in seclusion or near a special natural feature (an arbor or water feature is perfect) or Nature altar constructed especially for honoring Nature.

HABITAT ATTRACTION

As much as possible, welcome wildlife into your sanctuary setting. Most people who take the step to create their yard, garden, courtyard, patio, or balcony as a Nature sanctuary quickly discover a whole new relationship with the many creatures who come and go. You, too, can learn to provide, through vegetation and other means, the type of food, water, shelter, and nesting space for a wide diversity of insects and larger animals. Laying fear aside for curiosity, you can learn that it is this very diversity of wildlife in a Nature haven that provides its own checks and balances, where a type of harmony exists between species.

So imagine, if you will, meandering pathways, garden art that breathes new life into a flower bed, filtered sunlight warming a small pond with a tiny tree frog croaking out its exuberant song, and a butterfly sunning itself on a nearby rock. Imagine a chair or bench that enfolds your body and spirit in a state of being instead of doing. Whatever you can imagine, you can begin to create it. Don't worry about your low budget or lack of space or the need to ration out your precious free time. Those thoughts are the too familiar symptoms of the disease of adulthood.

Re-enchantment with the Nature outside your own back door will inspire you to find the niches of creative time wherein the process of soul-building and soil-building become one. Here the practical and spiritual are unified, and you pass over a threshold into a new way of perceiving everyday life. Like the curious children who climbed into the wardrobe in C. S. Lewis's childhood classic, *The Lion, the Witch, and the Wardrobe*, you will suddenly find yourself in a magical land of possibilities. Just allow your curiosity to be greater than your fear. Let your heart supercede your doubts. As the famous Greek novelist, Nikos Kazantzakis, reminds us, "The new earth exists only in the heart." Be alert—you *do* need daily sanctuary. Your heart and soul depend upon it.

THE NEED FOR SOLITUDE, STILLNESS, AND REFLECTION

The soul has an inherent need for balance. Compelled to *do,* it desires worldly immersion and enchantment, but the soul also needs to know it can just *be.* This *being* means occasional retreat from the frontlines of life—retreat into solitude, stillness, and reflection.

A Sanctuary Garden allows both doing and being to find natural balance in its Keeper. However, the design of a Sanctuary Garden especially incorporates opportunities to just *be.* Special sitting areas are important. So are meandering paths. Central landscape features such as a waterfall, pond, tree, or rock formation are each important in drawing a visitor to sit quietly in observation. Lastly, a hidden room or nook in the garden is perfect for soliciting solitude and reflection.

What is it like to just *be?* In *Sisters of the Earth,* a collection of women's prose and poetry about Nature, editor Lorraine Anderson talks about "making a conscious choice to slow down to seed time or rock time, to still the clamoring ego, to set aside plans and busyness, and simply to be present in my body, to offer myself up." How can we offer ourselves up to the subtle rhythmic sway and flow of Nature? Can this really be done in a society in which overworked or stressed-out individuals perform all their duties without ever once planting foot on terra firma from the time they leave their home to the time they return? Perhaps the secret is in taking small steps toward creating opportunities for stillness and contemplation. Just a few minutes here and there—to breathe more deeply, to think more slowly, to perceive Nature around us with greater awareness, or perhaps to perceive the world within our soul.

What if we begin by placing a single chair or bench outside so that it faces a small flower bed in our yard, a special tree, or even a seasonal planter? I met a young man recently who, in absence of a garden, has tendered a small potted plant on his bedroom window sill for years. With warmth in his eyes, he shared with me that *this* was his Sanctuary Garden. He sat before the

AN OLD FAMILIAR REFUGE
FOR THE SOUL

plant in a few minutes of silence each day, quietly noticing a new leaf node here or a flower bud there. There is a lesson here—to give ourselves permission to sit as often as possible before a bit of Nature without judging ourselves as to the time duration—to offer our attention unconditionally. Season by season, we can observe the same scene, letting it teach us through its subtle shifting.

When I was a new mother, my partner and I left the city, taking our two-month-old son and moving to a wild piece of property on the Olympic Peninsula in Washington. Miles from civilization, we lived contentedly in a tiny cabin with a dirt floor. On the crudely built deck that literally hung over the edge of a steep little valley, I placed a single planter box, fashioned from an old wooden crate. Because our garden space was to be carved out of a deep thicket of alders, and much water had to be hauled by hand to water it, I contented myself in the early stages with this one-planter garden full of bright annual flowers. I sat for hours, nursing my son, gazing across the valley, and admiring my flower box and its daily growth. It was one of the happiest periods of my life, where I was utterly content to be still, reflecting on the miraculous new life in my arms, in the beauty of Nature around me, and in my synthesis of human and Nature, as reflected perfectly in my simple little flower box.

I fully expect to return someday to such a one-planter garden with full awareness that it is the consciousness we bring to our Sanctuary Garden—no matter how large or small—that magnifies its incredible power to heal the lonely or broken heart and still the weary mind. Where is that special form of Nature that beckons you into being still and thankful for life?

THE NEED FOR REVERENT COMMUNION AND CELEBRATION

The soul is empowered by deep and meaningful relationships, be they with people, animals, plants, objects, or beautiful sunsets. The Sanctuary Garden is a special place where reverential stewardship is practiced between humans and Nature. Therefore, in our garden we can demonstrate a commitment to earth-friendly attitudes and actions. Being a reverent Keeper represents that added level of conscientious planning and caretaking necessary to make the garden feel worthy of sacredness and communion.

The reciprocal exchange between human and Nature is one of the most profound experiences to be had. This is communion at its deepest core—when, as theologian and ecologist Thomas Berry suggests, we perceive "the numinous quality of every earthly reality." A covenant of reverence with Nature is what allows each of us to feel part of Her mystique and to celebrate Her mystery. It allows us to use that part of our soul that historian Theodore Roszak calls our *rhapsodic intellect.*

Nobel laureate and scientist Barbara McClintock speaks eloquently of this form of rhapsodic mystique in her work with corn cells: "I found the more I worked with them, the bigger and bigger the chromosomes got and when I was really working with them I wasn't outside. I was part of the system . . . and these were my friends. As you look at these things they become a part of you . . . [such that] everytime I walk on grass I feel sorry because I know the grass is screaming at me." This is the type of communion that writer and poet Gretel Ehrlich writes about when she says "I must first offer myself up, accept all that comes before me."

Repeatedly, Forrest and I suggest that the Sanctuary Garden, perhaps more so than any other type of garden, is a link to the Divine, some indescribable Creative Force. In such a garden spiritual communion and celebration come easily because the garden quenches something so much more needed by the soul than intellectual preoccupation with horticultural techniques or manipulation of plants and the environment.

Indeed, we can see into and relate to the world and our life with eyes wide and accepting. Whether we commune with Nature with unspoken intuition or informed knowledge, we remain humble to the sacredness of our reverential covenant and relationship with Her. This form of transcendent wisdom cannot be gained in gardening books or at nurseries. It is gained on one's brown-stained knees or in the still observation of a subtle shift of energy in the air, within the soil or drop of rain, or emitted by an insect, rock, or plant. As Albert Einstein reminds us, "The most beautiful emotion we can experience is the mystical. It is the sower of all true art and science. He to whom this emotion is a stranger is as good as dead." If anything, your Sanctuary Garden can give you daily rebirth into the realms of the seen and unseen of Nature and your soul.

THE NEED FOR RE-CREATION & CO-CREATION

Our spiritual energy needs to be renewed each day. Our soul needs to be uplifted, and our wounded or tired spirit needs periodic regeneration. Finding sanctuary in a lovely and peaceful garden setting—one that seems to enfold the soul in magic, celebration, art, curiosity, and contemplation—can do the job. However, this is a big departure from our cultural stereotypes of recreation: television, sports, window shopping, going to the mall or a lounge. While there may be a place for all this, perhaps in our quest for a balanced life we might consider asking ourselves, which activities and experiences truly nurture and renew us on the deepest level?

I am still amazed at how much time I managed to waste in the past with unnecessary activities and pursuits. However, all the while I was sincerely honing my discrimination and my inner life and vision. So, I have no real regrets, but I think more carefully now before leaving the calmness of our sanctuary to drive into town.

To co-create with Nature has become the highest and most regenerating activity I can perform. It has deepened my power as a woman and set the standard for all other relationships in my life. The very act of co-creation asks that we listen constantly to the voices around us. They seem to guide us wordlessly, intuitively, in fostering the right relationships and balance of plants to natural features, of wildlife habitat to human haven, of what is left wild and what must be cultivated.

I did not learn any of this in gardening books I am sad to say. My garden is my library of natural history whose plants, insects, beings, and forces make up the many volumes that command my attention each visit. Forrest reminds me that Nature is awash in storytelling and, so often, in our need as gardeners to constantly be busy and in control we choose not to listen to the stories. In his journal, Forrest writes: "There is a universe little known in the earth at our feet. We talk much more than rocks have the patience to listen."

Each of us evolves philosophically, enriched by or orphaned from our relationship with Nature, as we choose. Every aspect of Nature, truly seen and felt through the gesture of reverence, has the power to lead us back to the sanctuary of our soul. In *Sisters of the Earth,* Gretel Ehrlich reminds us: "To trace the history of a river, or a raindrop, as John Muir would have done, is also to trace the history of the soul, the history of the mind descending and arising in the body. In both we constantly seek and stumble on divinity, which, like the cornice feeding the lake and the spring becoming a waterfall, feeds, spills, falls, and feeds itself over and over again."

What, then, is really the value of seeking sanctuary in daily life? Whether it be in meditation, a quiet corner of a room in the house, or in the garden, finding refuge refuels our sense of spirit. We also know that in sanctuary we can perceive greater control in our life. We can love ourselves anew by embracing our sacredness. We re-envision the world as, perhaps, a more hopeful and peaceful place in which to live. In sanctuary, we often become re-enchanted with beauty. We create a sacred connection with Nature, and we deepen those values we hold dear in a worthy relationship. Sanctuary naturally develops our spiritual side, but it also allows us to perceive our sense of service to others, and to embrace their sacredness with more clarity, love, and compassion. Finally, the gentle power of sanctuary does wonders to restore our peace of mind, perhaps the greatest gift that taking sacred time and space can give to us. In sanctuary that elusive peace we seek in all aspects of our life seems more easily attainable.

Now we will share some of the specific design elements we feel are key to creating a Sanctuary Garden. Each has a very practical side and also a spiritual justification. We believe this is the way gardening should be: an opportunity to grow soulfully, while rooted in reverence for this planet Earth we call our home. To borrow from an old Scottish saying: "Love this Earth as if you won't be here tomorrow; show reverence for your Garden as if you will be here forever."

3

The Entrance

A garden which can only be reached

through a series of outer gardens keeps its secrecy.

—CHRISTOPHER ALEXANDER,

A Pattern Language

$\mathcal{T}$*he secret of a Sanctuary Garden* lies in part in its mystery, and this mystery must be accessed at a special point and in a special way—the entrance. The entrance to a Sanctuary Garden can be one of its most powerful features. As more than a location the entrance is an opportunity to check in with your soul—the need for sanctuary, the willingness to surrender worldly cares, the consideration of properly humble, appreciative, and reverent behavior.

Thomas Moore, in *The Re-enchantment of Everyday Life,* reminds us, "Entering a garden is like passing through a mystical gate. Things are not the same on the other side." What if we treated our garden's entrance as if it, too, were a garden, a type of *outer garden* that keeps the rest of the Sanctuary Garden veiled and mysteriously just out of full view?

Truly, if your garden is a sacred place in your life, it is deserving of a thoughtfully designed entrance. Your Sanctuary Garden proper may even be seen as a type of inner sanctum to be accessed by passages and levels—a series of outer gardens. The entrance and its accompanying threshold, therefore, is one such space that, as you pass through it, gradually intensifies and converges on the garden site. Like a gracious host anticipating your arrival the entrance is where the garden befriends you, *allowing* you to enter.

Many gardens do not have a formal entrance or even a gate. In fact my first gardens did not have a proper entrance. Why? Probably because for all those years, a garden, after all, was more a kind of outdoor pantry than anything else. It was purely a practical endeavor. As I travel and consult with others who need advice or direction in planning their garden, I am not surprised to hear similiar views, which reflect my own experience. Now, however, when a person asks me where to begin in seeking sanctuary in their yard or garden, I suggest the creation of an entrance—a specific

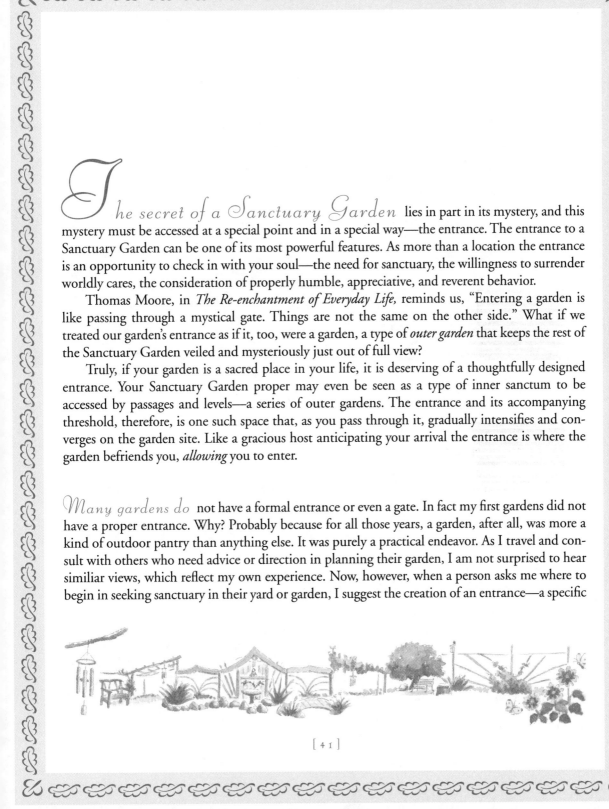

The Psychology of an Effective Entrance

· A feeling of *safe haven* is created as the visitor crosses over the entrance threshold from the world outside into the sanctuary of the garden.
· Feeling welcomed and enfolded by natural and artful features, the visitor is easily induced to leave his or her worries and cares at the entrance.
· The visitor's imagination is engaged, creating a state of receptivity and curiosity. There is an inherent need to wonder, "What lies ahead?"
· Plantings, sounds, sitting areas, and other artful and natural objects allow the visitor to pause and better appreciate subtleties along the entrance threshold.
· The feeling of comfort at this form of *outer garden* entrance is impressed upon the visitor's mind and more easily guides the journey into the further reaches of the garden.
· The visitor feels as if his or her personal well-being was carefully considered by the garden's Keeper. It is much easier, therefore, to surrender to peace and inner tranquility.

spot that you *pass through,* as if it were a veil that separates your refuge from the hubbub of the world.

Although, over the years I was slowly beginning to discover my own brand of gardening theology, the sacredness of gardens and gardening had not yet occurred to me. Therefore, I entered each of my gardens wherever, whenever convenience dictated: precisely at the row in which I would be weeding or planting or watering. Simple as that.

I never lived in any one place for more than a gardening season or two, so my gardens were only brief waysides. I did not develop that deeper sense of rootedness and connection to place that might have inspired in me an art more reverent than the mere shaping of planting beds, and carving out straight paths that marked the quickest way from point A to point B. Now, however, I feel different.

When you are ready to create a special place—your Sanctuary Garden—you suddenly notice subtle details that never before seemed important. You discover the marvelous interconnectedness of rocks and plants, color and lighting, water and wind sounds, and wildlife. The Earth calls out to you for partnership in a way you have never experienced. Don't let an opportunity like this go by.

The Entrance

Much as I have entered into a devoted, lifelong partnership with Forrest through our marriage, when I enter our garden I do so in a similar spirit of dedication to a co-creative partnership with Nature.

A friend stopped by one day with her Mayan visitor, Jorge. When Jorge appeared at our garden's entrance I was astonished when he rolled his pants above his knees and knelt to kiss the earth. My friend later told me that this is a Mayan custom when entering a garden or field. This simple reverent gesture moved me so deeply that I have never since seen entrances in quite the same way.

To enter a place with a full sense of consciousness not only empowers our own reverent spirit, but it also empowers the place and the spirit of the place itself. Have you ever entered your garden in such a way—with such honor and humility? Have you ever conceived of your relationship to the Earth as one of service, so much so that, as you stand at your garden's side you hear a voice within ask, "Beloved Earth, what are *Your* needs today?"

I can only imagine that Jorge's bow was a way to uphold a sacred relationship he had entered into long ago as a child in the Mayan forests and fields surrounding his village. Wherever he travelled, he walked on the Earth and touched Her countenance as if for the first time, seeking Her good graces. Mayan culture sees in the Earth one's tether to the Divine. To be allowed to enter our

How to Enter with Soul

- Pause for a moment and collect your thoughts.
- Prepare to make the transition from outside activities and concerns to only those of peace and reverence.
- Consider your needs for sanctuary and how this special place reflects those needs.
- Be considerate of the needs of Nature in this haven. Ask this simple question, "How can I serve Thee as I am myself served?"
- Admire the purity of intention of this sanctuary as reflected by the Keeper's partnership with Nature.
- Thank God for being alive.
- "Close the gate" behind you and walk with gratitude for all living things, within this sanctuary and without.

garden was to uphold a reciprocal sacred bond based on unconditionality and trust. Jorge was saying "If I am allowed to enter, then how can I serve Thee?"

This more *spiritual* view of entering the garden has only come to me more recently. As with Tricia, the garden was what lay just outside the back door. I passed by it or through it. I did not give much thought about *entering* it. The fence kept intruders out and the vegetables and flowers in (as if they were hell-bent on storming the walls anyway). And the gate or entrance? Simply an exterior door hanging on rusty hinges about which I always wondered, lying in bed at night, if I remembered to close and lock it.

Now, when I reflect on the several entrances our garden has had over the years—each reflecting the garden's expansion and our own spiritual evolution—I think of the *principle of rightness* that has permeated the process. Much of our satisfaction or discomfort with choices in our life comes about by assessing how right something feels on a gut level. We may think, Does this relationship feel right? Is this the right place and time? Does this spiritual path seem right for me? All of these questions have entrance points into the evolution of our soul—a gate or door leading us into yet another room or period of time and exploration in our life. Think of your soul as a garden, and you are faced with just how to enter it every day to nurture it. How you do so must feel right *to you*.

At one time, our tiny garden resembled a prison compound, surrounded by field fencing and barbed wire. That was the garden we inherited from the previous owner. We entered it by pulling back a flap of wire fencing. Then, several years later, the garden was significantly enlarged, and we created a more formal batwing gate made of two-by-fours and one-inch lath. A geometric pattern based on straight lines, like the rays of a sun turned sideways, greeted visitors and kept deer out. It took a few years for me to realize what didn't seem right about this entrance—too clever, and the lines were too straight, like an exercise in Geometry 101. The lines of Nature are much softer and more fluid. Luckily, the garden was enlarged again, and I had my chance to do it right. But, this time, over seven years after that first wire fence, I felt inspired by a Nature that had rooted like a spiritual teacher within my soul.

When you begin to think about the entrance to your Sanctuary Garden, consider what feels right to you. Is it in the right place, will it have a form and appearance that feels right? Is it fulfilling its purpose? A recent visit to a friend's house validated just what I am talking about. To the side of her house stood the bare wooden frame of a gate and several fence posts. She said it had been like that for months now. She felt unresolved about what type of statement she wanted this key entrance to her garden to make. Eventually, she will surrender to what feels right for her. At least she is giving her entrance its full due consideration.

I strongly believe, after numerous garden entrances under my belt, that there is more to an entrance than just a gate or arch or narrow opening of shrubs for the body to pass through. In the mystical sense of the term, this is the door your consciousness passes through each step of the way. I am sure my friend was thinking about this very thing. The Navajo concept, *Hakomi,* reminds us

to consider "Where do I stand in relationship to these things?" And that is exactly what entering our garden, home, or the open arms of our partner, friend, or child asks us to consider.

To gently stimulate this passage of consciousness, we have now created our entrance as a long threshold, perhaps over fifty feet in length. This outer garden chamber keeps visitors there for a while, giving them time to relax and unwind. No hurry. This is spiritual time. There's eternity here in a flower, a beckoning bench, or the sound of water. And in this outer garden, there is a type of healing and soothing beginning to take place.

It is true, as Forrest describes, that our garden's entrance has changed and become more artful and purposeful as we have deepened. But, regardless of the actual form, the *feeling* for me when approaching our garden's entrance is one of deep gratitude. When I am returning after spending hours in town, I drive down the long winding driveway until I see the garden entrance: the wooden arch, the woven hazelnut fence and gate, the cedar birdhouse on a post, the carved wooden sign overhead reading "Spirit and Nature Dancing Together."

As I get out of the car and walk toward the entrance I feel my exhaustion and the accumulated tension of the city and traffic begin to fall away. Already I am breathing more slowly and deeply. I open the gate and pass through a lovely threshold, overwhelmed with gratitude for this beautiful, safe place that gives me so much peace and think again of the words of Thomas Moore: "In a garden the soul finds its needed escape from life and its entry into a space where eternity is more evident than time and where the ritual arrangement of life is more important than the business of surviving and making progress."

Stand with me for a few minutes just inside the garden's entrance. Let me take you on a journey in your mind's eye:

Imagine, if you will, taking a last look back as you close the wooden latch of the gate. The city, the road, your car, *and* your cares are all left behind, easily forgotten in the present moment awareness of the natural and human handicraft that surrounds you. Your well-being is our concern and, as proper hosts, we have made your visit and friendship our highest priority, right here at the entrance.

NESTLED AMONG RHODODENDRONS DAISIES JAPANESE ANEMONE & FRAGRANT LILIES OF THE VALLEY, THIS SHADY WHIMSICAL BENCH FOR ONE LOOKS OUT UPON THE WATERFALL NEAR THE ENTRANCE

Casually gaze about. Planters of various sizes sit on either side of the stone path. They are filled with bright flowers. The planting bed on the right, along the west side of our cedar-shingled house, though it receives almost no sun, is filled with bright-leaved plants. There are green and yellow variegated acuba shrubs, delicate ground covers of green and silver-leaved lamiums with dainty pink and yellow flowers, bicolor hostas, and a drift of foxglove and columbine, among others. Enfolded in these simple plantings, not more than five or six feet from the gate, is a small bench Forrest made from a salvaged piece of cedar slab from a downed tree he found in town. It, along with the whimsical ceramic sculpture my son, Oceah, made, are sitting on one end of the bench, beckoning you to sit. Feel the shrubs gently brush your shoulders and arms, almost as if offering to massage your soul.

Sitting now, you breathe deeply and notice the other side of the path. You wonder, "Have all these plants always been here? They seem so natural. And how is it I overlooked that interesting piece of driftwood vertically rising and facing the gate with limbs resembling open arms? And just opposite it a silver basin of polished river stones submerged in water, almost asking me to partake in a finger bath to remove the city residue from my skin? And, my goodness, standing next to the pedasteled basin, is that what I think it is—a type of coat rack naturally shaped from an old dead madrone branch, like a welcoming butler offering to take my heavy worldly cloak?"

Our entrance clearly is not meant to overwhelm you. If you sit long enough you begin to focus anew, to gain perspective. It is your choice. We merely encourage the visitor to surrender to peace. And, here at the outer hearth of our garden, is exactly the right place to touch your vulnerable spirit.

Across from the bench more interesting colors and textures brighten another dark area where little sun touches. But the large rhododendrons, native to Oregon forests, and the green and purple hypericum bushes with their sequence of bright yellow flowers and purple berries—these gain your attention, too. Woodland flowers cascade over the high bank—prunella, columbine, lamb's ear, tiarella, violets, lovely bloodroots, cyclamen, and others. These plants have naturalized here at the entrance almost effortlessly, receiving no maintenance but the appreciative gaze of a passing pilgrim. Even the lowly sow thistle that intermingles with the tapestry is welcome for a while in spring, until it is mature enough to be easily pulled as succulent fodder for our rabbits. Partly hidden in the foliage, an old wicker stool sits like a forgotten dais, once well-used but now a rustic symbol of relaxation. On a mossy stump sits a large iridescent raw opal, symbolizing the refracting light of our soul as it is reflected in the play of life and all its colorful possibilities.

From where you sit, imagine you are hidden deep within a many-chambered nautilus shell. Sights, sounds, textures, fragrances easily resonate within your soul. The musk you cannot place actually rises from beneath your feet, emanating from the Corsican mint on the path near the bench, and which you unknowingly stepped on when entering. Behind you is the gentle tinkling of a handcrafted wind chime made of thin slices of polished rock—the duller sound is not as obtrusive as metal in this location. The cedar slab bench itself is purposely rough, partly a by-product of the milling process from its mother tree, but also to draw your hand to its surface.

Still sitting, you also hear the soothing sound of a small waterfall. From some undetermined location, it greets you and then, as you look ahead, you see it emerging from a wild thicket of giant sword ferns, rock, fragrant daphne, and other natural woodland shrubs backed by large fir trees, two quaking aspens, and a golden tree peony. Native bleeding hearts, other ferns, lilies-of-the-valley, snowberry, wild iris, huckleberry—all seem to flow out of the forest fringe like a throng of children rushing out to greet a newcomer to their playground.

The Sanctuary Garden

You feel at ease in this natural setting. It all seems to have grown naturally and effortlessly out of the Earth. The sunlight gently filters down through the dense forest canopy. Birds are singing, and two tiny tree frogs croak from the pond, one voice high and one low. The path meanders to the left past a small deck and yet another small bench nearer the water, and continues up the gentle slope toward the main garden. It feels good to just sit and collect your thoughts, and to let the cool water sounds and the gentle breeze through the firs cleanse and calm you. You have gone no more than 15 feet from the gate. Something has already changed within. Welcome to our sanctuary.

Poet Gary Snyder says, "We have no one to teach us which parts of the landscape were once thought to be sacred, but with much time and attention, I think we will be able to identify such sites again."

It certainly is not necessary to think that sacred landscape is always somewhere other than the earth at our feet or that which is flourishing in our garden. Our garden becomes sacred by the ways in which we approach it—the purity of our intentions and needs when we stand at the entrance. And our perception of what Nature, through our garden, calls out for us to do for Her as well.

For Tricia and I, this is exactly what the symbolic and spiritual power of a Sanctuary Garden's entrance must evoke: a nostalgic, nonverbal *remembering* of what our bond with Nature, this Earth, and the Divine is all about. Our Sanctuary Garden, therefore, ceases to be just another safe place within the world yet removed from secular life. She becomes our teacher in matters of peace, courtesy, and stewardship of place.

Every day I step out of the safety of our home and into the abode of Nature and our garden. My first gesture is to squat low to the Earth, touch the ground with my palm, bring some rich soil to my nostrils, and offer myself to the day in service. Consider for the moment that the air of this Earth is free for the taking as is the warmth of the sunlight and the freshness of rain. Remembering this only takes a moment of our time. Doing so grounds us to this Earth, not just to our cars and our careers, our highways and aspirations. Try pausing in the same place every day and make that your entrance into the Divine. Stand or sit there for a few moments and focus your attention on your own essence as a sacred being in search of peace. In time that very spot will be charged by your presence and you by it. It will become, as in Austalian aborigine lore, a "dreaming" spot. And what better dream than to remember your connection to the Divine and to the Earth?

Here at Cortesia, we have tried to accomplish several key things at our entrance without being obvious or contrived about it. First of all, we want you to be sufficiently intrigued so that you will *want* to slow down, in fact stop, so that you won't miss anything. We also want you to

dream a little bit, to remember the peace or awe and wonder you once knew as a child, for example, at play in tall grassy fields, among flower beds, or alongside creeks.

As you carefully look around you will see miniversions of all the key features of a Sanctuary
Garden—a sitting area, a water feature, and interesting color and lighting, from the shade of deep
forest to mottled sunlight to a strong sunset glow later in the day as it reflects off the house and
surrounding foliage. Clearly, you are in a natural setting that welcomes wild creatures, yet garden
art and human touches capture your attention fifteen feet inside the entrance. Natural features
such as wood, moss-covered rocks, and vine-woven fencing seem a timeless and organic part of the
environment. An inviting wooden deck off the back porch offers you a choice of seating, from a
simple bench to adjustable back chairs to a deluxe rocking chair from which to view the watercourse and small pond.

The mood here is relaxed, but you don't see plastic, mislaid objects, hoses, and the like. The sounds of water, windchimes, birds, and wind entice your mind to wander in reverie. Indeed, the world has receded too far away for you to even care. Your car, after all, is already far out of sight up the driveway and in the meadow on the other side of a thick bank of trees and shrubs.

What we have actually succeeded in doing is to *elongate* the effect of the entrance. We have invited you into our dream of the Earth. Thus, we have heightened and magnified several psychological benefits of a thoughtful garden entrance. These include the following:

Ten Tips on Creating Your Sanctuary Garden Entrance

Guiding Thoughts: Allow your own unique personality to be reflected in the design of your sanctuary entrance. Let your ideas evolve and your entrance be open to change. With your sensitive direction, your entrance will be a soulful expression that brings your visitors the memory of their own soul-nature.

1. *Enclosure.* A nice entrance is enhanced by the feeling of a sense of enclosure around your designated sanctuary space. The enclosure can be formal, as with a fence, or implied, as with a grouping of shrubs or even potted plants acting as visual screens.

2. *Fencing.* Strive to make a fence or wall as natural as possible, especially near the entrance. Avoid barbed wire, chain link, field fencing, and the like. Natural wood, branches, bamboo, wrought iron or other artistic metalwork, a live hedge, or even a long trellis separating the garden from the outside shows creative sensitivity.

3. *Archways.* Arched entrances are powerful passages that greatly accentuate the drama of the entrance threshold. They can be created with posts and wood beams, curving branches, wrought iron, vines, or perhaps the leafy branches of a tree that one walks beneath.

4. *Gates.* A gate should be well-conceived and reflect your personality. Decide if you want it to be solid, blocking the view in, or more open, thus offering a glimpse of the garden within. Here is an opportunity to be artistic and creative. Make sure the latch is efficient and easy to use. A gate or archway is also a good place to hang a sanctuary sign, an inspiring quote, or welcoming thought, or even the name of your Sanctuary Garden.

5. *Potted Plants.* Draw attention above the ground at or near your entrance with

· You feel welcomed and enfolded into a special place.
· It is easy to leave your worries and cares at the gate.
· Your imagination is engaged, creating a state of receptivity, curiosity, and anticipation of what lies ahead.
· You are encouraged to pause, so as to better appreciate the subtleties along the way.
· You easily feel comfortable, almost as if you were a guest of honor.
· You truly feel a sense of safe haven, which makes it easier to let peace permeate your soul.

clusters of large and small potted flowers or planter boxes. They can be changed seasonally and should be kept attractive. This works just as well for a balcony garden or a tiny backyard as it does for a larger garden space. You can even pot a small tree to create a little shade and vertical interest in an entrance that otherwise lacks vegetation.

6. *Focal Points*. Create interest at your entrance's threshold that allows the visitor to pause. This could include some very large-leaved plants, an artful bench, a large boulder, a special piece of garden art or sculpture, a water feature, a specimen tree or shrub, seasonal flower planters, the framing of a view ahead, even a basket of inspirational quote cards.

7. *Lighting*. Consider the right type of natural lighting to accentuate your entrance— bright sun, filtered, or mostly shade. These options are key in establishing a mood. The addition of night lighting around the entrance, along the path, or by spotlighting a particular feature not only provides an aura of safety but it also encourages evening visits to the garden.

8. *Colored Plantings*. If your entrance has low natural lighting (shade), incorporate some brighter-leaved plants; yellow, white, or pastel flowers; and garden art that is light-colored (such as concrete statues or a ceramic bird bath).

9. *Sitting Area*. Entice the visitor to sit near the entrance so as to take in this form of outer garden. Let the bench or chair reflect your personality and artistic sensibility.

10. *Pathways*. As much as possible, let any pathway leading up to and beyond the entrance be meandering and winding rather than always straight. This creates intrigue, and can make the garden feel more spacious as well as more relaxed. If straight paths are unavoidable, conceal them by making the path itself artistic—stepping stones, mossy interplantings, different textures of pebbles, level changes, and so on. Additionally, let plants creep over and into the path out of their side borders naturally—this creates the illusion of a varied pathway.

Obviously, we have given a great deal of thought to our entrance, as we have to the rest of our garden. You might have to forgive our impassioned efforts and ideals as you now focus on your own setting. Perhaps your Sanctuary Garden is a small courtyard or patio, or even the balcony of a second-floor apartment. Perhaps it is a special place tucked behind a screen of shrubs, or a favorite outdoor chair sitting beneath a stately maple or wisteria arbor. Maybe it is contained somewhere in your vegetable garden, tucked in a corner near a fence or trellis. And, if you are fortunate or highly motivated, maybe your Sanctuary Garden *is* the larger part of your backyard showcased through the large picture window of your living room.

Of course, the choice is up to you. Remember, the entrance is only one component of a Sanctuary Garden. You are not obligated to give any thought to it at all. Instead, you might desire to focus on one or more other design elements and still feel a sense of *sanctuary* in your garden. Still and all, you understand now the symbolism of an entrace and its psychological effects. Let's now look at how you can specifically shape your own unique entrance.

Based upon our own experience and many years of observing and assisting others in the creation of their gardens, we have identified six components of an entrance to think about. These include:

- Structure
- Path
- View
- Lighting
- Plants
- Art

STRUCTURE

The actual physical structure of an entrance, while not absolutely necessary, gives it an appearance and feel of *permanence* and *groundedness*. In every season of the year, even when plants have died back and trees and shrubs may be bare, a solid arch, trellis, gate, or framed entryway of some kind is always there to usher the visitor into your sanctuary.

Gardens in general need the consistency of structure to balance the everchanging appearance and disappearance of plant and animal life. But almost nowhere, in our view, is this more important than at the entrance. If a sitting area or bench is also placed near your entrance threshold, this will provide an additional stabilizing influence, as well as encouraging the quiet observation of life in the garden no matter what the time of year.

Even the posting of a carved wooden sign above or next to your entrance lends an element of solidity and meaning. The very recognition of the name, or perhaps an inspiring quote that is offered there, is a tether to the process of honoring the spirit and intention of the Sanctuary Garden that lies beyond.

If you use an arched entrance—one like the many you might see at garden centers—please do not skimp on quality. Natural wood, such as cedar or redwood, is long-lasting, and quality archways are functional and show their artistic craftsmanship well. Vining foliage always appear to be embedded in the design, and once the arched trellis is covered with vegetation it creates a natural sense of entrance *and* enclosure. A few years ago, our friend Elizabeth added a series of three large wooden arches at the front of her garden, which faces the street. Now the vines and plants growing on and around these structures are mature and the front yard is somewhat hidden and much more private.

When considering gates think about height, width, ease of opening and closing, and the all-important solid or see-through issue. The two gates at Cortesia are constructed of a cedar frame and the top of each is a naturally arched, debarked fir limb. Their see-through quality, however, is what captures the imagination and appreciation of visitors. The gates are actually woven wild-hazelnut switches and create an interesting stained-glass effect. The gates have excellent tinsel strength, and infrequently broken switches can be easily replaced. We opted for a transparent entrance, so as to tease the approaching visitor with glimpses into the outer garden. Furthermore, the drama of our expansive country setting does not fit well with the idea of trying to shut it behind solid wood gates.

High, nontransparent gates, however, can create that "secret garden" effect, and may fit well for a setting that itself is enclosed in a high wooded or cinder block fence or wall. Let your sense of what *feels right* be expressed in a way that enhances both your garden's entrance and enclosure.

PATH

The width and direction of the path into the garden or entrance threshold will also have a major influence on the view ahead. A somewhat narrow and meandering path will generally cause more of the garden to be hidden at any given time. Taller shrubs, or one or more small trees such as Japanese maple, when placed near the entrance on either side of the path will create a feeling of intimacy and help confine the attention to the area closest at hand.

In small yards, we see more and more the creation of a network of curving paths amidst dense and carefully layered plantings. This works really well to create the illusion of a much larger garden. Wandering back and forth, here and there, you could easily spend an hour or two and still not see everything. This effect can be started right at the entrance.

At Cortesia, the path is fairly straight and wide near the entrance, because it is deep shade and we want to create a brighter, more open feeling. But, as you proceed through our elongated threshold, you notice plants spilling over banks and borders, and large mossy rocks sitting

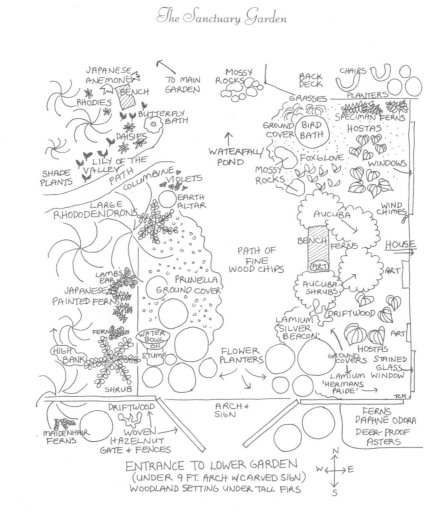

JAPANESE ANEMONE
TO MAIN GARDEN
BENCH
RHODIES
BUTTERFLY BATH
DAISIES
LILY OF THE VALLEY
SHADE PLANTS
PATH
COLUMBINE
VIOLETS
EARTH ALTAR
LARGE RHODODENDRONS
LAMBS EAR
PRUNELLA GROUND COVER
JAPANESE PAINTED FERNS
FERNS
WATER BOWL ON STUMP
HIGH BANK
SHRUB
MAIDENHAIR FERNS
DRIFTWOOD
WOVEN HAZELNUT GATE & FENCES

MOSSY ROCKS
BACK DECK
CHAIRS
PLANTERS
GRASSES
SPECIMAN FERNS
GROUND COVER
BIRD BATH
HOSTAS
WATERFALL POND
FOXGLOVE
WINDOWS
MOSSY ROCKS
WIND CHIMES
AUCUBA
BENCH
FERNS
HOUSE
ART
PATH OF FINE WOOD CHIPS
ART
AUCUBA SHRUBS
DRIFTWOOD
LAMIUM 'SILVER BEACON'
ART
FLOWER PLANTERS
HOSTAS
GROUND COVERS
STAINED GLASS WINDOW
LAMIUM 'HERMANS PRIDE'
ARCH + SIGN
FERNS
DAPHNE ODORA
DEER-PROOF ASTERS

ENTRANCE TO LOWER GARDEN
(UNDER 9 FT. ARCH W/CARVED SIGN)
WOODLAND SETTING UNDER TALL FIRS

N
W — E
S

encroaching the path. The visitor's attention is drawn away from an otherwise wide and straight path over fifteen feet in length before it naturally begins to narrow and curve leftward up a gentle slope toward the garden. The path itself, made of decomposing, finely chipped wood, is soft underfoot.

The entryway is a perfect place for some special rockwork, artful stepping-stones, tiles, or even small, round gravel with larger rocks in between or as an edging. Very low-growing ground-covers such as creeping thymes, Corsican mint, baby tears, blue star creeper, monk's grass, or Irish moss can also be integrated into a path, entryway, or courtyard. Just be sure the stepping-stones are properly placed so that the plants don't get trampled too much.

VIEW

The view from your sanctuary entrance is an important aspect to consider. Giving just a glimpse of what is ahead adds to the mystery and allure. This strategy serves to stimulate the curiosity of your guests without taking away from the drama and interest of the entrance itself. A simple principle is *one thing at a time.* If visitors (and you, too) can see the entire garden at a glance, they may be drawn into the main part before they have fully taken in and appreciated the entrance threshold—an outer garden unto itself. One view you do not want to have is that of disarray: misplaced hoses, tools, empty pots, debris piles, and the like. No one should have to look at any of these items as part of their first impression of your Sanctuary Garden.

Of course, it is entirely possible that your Sanctuary Garden is entered into immediately upon passing through a gate, arch, or narrow passage created by shrubs or other vegetation. Or perhaps a full-fledged view of your garden is had from the confines of your living room. If this is the case, then you have many options at your hand to comfort the visitor, including all the other design elements discussed in this book.

LIGHTING

While you may not feel that you have much or any control over the natural lighting that exists at your Sanctuary Garden's entrance, you can choose to enhance the type of lighting that *does* exist. For example, choosing plants with bright-leafed or varigated foliage (particularly with some yellow or white) will brighten a dark area.

If you actually want to create more shade, plant one or more low-growing trees (Japanese maples are a favorite choice) or pot some. The mottled light provided by shade trees is very soothing and pleasant. On hot days our visitors linger long in the cool, woodland setting of our entrance and outer garden before venturing up the path into the sunny main garden situated in a large meadow. However, you may choose to create just the opposite effect.

Night lighting, especially with a dimmer switch, is valuable at an entrance, providing a sense both of safety and intrigue. Unless security is a primary issue, the starkness of spotlights can be diffused by placing them within the foliage of trees, but not in such a manner that they shine directly into one's eyes. An old-fashioned wrought-iron lantern on a post at the entrance is inviting. Certain foliage or a strong natural feature like a rock or water, can be accented at ground level. And, of course, one can place accent lights along the path.

PLANTS

Plants at your garden's entrance are, of course, vital. They soften and bring to life whatever structural elements exist there. Trellised flowering vines that climb overhead—roses, clematis, wisteria, trumpet vine, honeysuckle, grapes, and passion vine, for example—lend a wonderful air of romance and nostalgia to the garden entrance.

Other useful plants to consider at or near the entrance are evergreen shrubs, which maintain their look year 'round. They can serve as a nice backdrop to any seasonal flower planters you desire to have there, as well. Always, the inclusion of some native plants appropriate to your climate or region will ease the mainteance requirements a bit, provide habitat for wildlife, and contribute to a more natural look. We prefer a more naturally planted entrance, with perhaps a few planters and pots, to one that suggests that you have just arrived at a nursery or garden center. Save your money—a few pots of flowers may be all that is needed. It is okay to keep it very simple.

ART

Last but not least, you might consider integrating some garden art into your entrance threshold. It is a great mood enhancer and can make up for seasonal gaps in your landscape. Our two-foot-high statue of Saint Francis is placed a little way outside our entrance. He stands on his own all winter long, and the rest of the year is surrounded by whatever plants can thrive in the deep shade.

Keep art pieces few but make their presence known—this is a good rule of thumb. We observed one Sanctuary Garden entrance with only Tibetan bells hanging overhead, almost asking for your hand to jingle them. A water bowl, specimen rock, or wooden piece; a bowl of angel cards for the taking; an artful urn, well-crafted bench; a wind chime; maybe just a vase of freshly cut or dried flowers sitting on a dais—each can add their own magic to the overall effect.

Fortunately, there is no set formula and no right or wrong with garden art. Like a butterfly flitting here and there, the whimsy of garden art is that it is forever movable and changeable, and it allows you to exercise and gracefully stretch your imagination, while serving to clarify your intent to create an inviting mood.

4

Water

It is a fascinating and provocative thought
that a body of water deserves to be considered
as an organism in its own right.

—LYALL WATSON, *Supernature*

"What joy did you receive today?"

"That I sat still in the garden and watched it rain.
And my soul fiercely received the soaking."

—MIASHA

There is a river that runs through our soul. It begins as a gleam in one's eye, a drop of rain, a bubbling spring of hope. It pours across the earth as adolescent streams of whimsy, growing and enlarging, reaching out to soil, root, rock, leaf—reaching out for friends, companionship, trust. Broadening its play, it molds and moves onward blindly in search of the Divine. Over waterfalls, into pools, rushing, pausing, reflecting, ceaselessly dancing with life—at times struggling with effort, at times simply flowing and playing. Longing. It dreams of the ocean. All beings—and rivers are but one—dream of the Ocean of Peace. Crossing the continent of matter, surrendering to the universe of Spirit. Home at last, awaiting the final transformation, to rise again into the Cloud of Love."

These words came to me one day when listening to my favorite piece of music: "Moldau" from Smetana's *Ma Vlast (My Fatherland),* his long epic tribute to his homeland. The song is about a river that begins as small droplets of rain and snow melt high up in the mountains; it continues to chronicle the river's journey to the sea. Of course, the song is about more than a river. It tells of the birth, life, and transformation of the soul from spirit to flesh and back to spirit again.

Sadly, in an era where we take water for granted, we have lost its sacred meaning as the fount of Spirit. Like oxygen, we assume water is not only abundant but always readily available. We are so focused upon it as a resource that we are blind to its power as a spiritual force. Yet we do not need to be spiritually inclined at all to acknowledge that water is the lifeblood of all that exists on Earth.

Water is key to sanctuary. Its sacred influence over human history is unmatched among all other natural forces. Water is vital to insuring that Earth is a safe haven for all beings. Provide it, and they will come: human, plant, animal, insect, even bacteria, all depend on water. Lose this vital force, and Earth becomes just another barren rock circling the sun.

Water in your Sanctuary Garden is one of the most important features you can provide. You need not be extravagant in your design. Even if you provide a water bowl, you will be richly satisfied for any effort you make to honor water in your setting.

Water is not just what comes out of a hose or faucet. Why, your own body is two-thirds full of *aqua vita,* and every plant or animal in your garden is itself comprised of as much as three-quarters water. It would not be inaccurate to say, therefore, that your garden *thirsts* for your compassionate presence as its Keeper.

Let's do something brave here. For the moment, let's imagine that water is valued in our culture for its full spiritual qualities. Even more courageous, let's suppose that water in our garden is a sacred element we honor—not just for its practical use, but for its value in nourishing the Spirit of the Garden and the soul of its Keeper.

To help you take this unexpected leap of faith, let me reiterate three basic principles Tricia and I have shared earlier about your role as your garden's Keeper. First, in the creation of your Sanctuary

Garden, you are establishing a partnership with Nature based on reverence and respect. This cocreative relationship, secondly, is deepened by the purity of intention expressed by you, the Keeper. Finally, with devotion and care, you elevate the consciousness and psychic energy of your garden to that of a sacred enclosure—a sacred place of peace that yokes human, Nature, and the Divine.

Given these principles, the water you choose to honor in your garden has inherent spiritual meaning. For this reason, you have re-connected with another deeper side of our human legacy with water. As philosophers, writers, gardeners, *and* humans, we have chosen to honor water's sacred qualities in the simple water features at Cortesia: well-placed birdbaths, bowls, ponds, watercourses, and the like. Even the gurgle of a desktop fountain soothes and stimulates the creative process while we each write. In short, each water feature is an opportunity to touch something primal to the soul.

Water for the Soul

Our human relationship with water is ripe with history and meaning. Here are a number of benefits you may feel from having water in your sanctuary. Of course, any spiritual symbolism is yours to interpret.

- Water—both its sound and sensation—is cleansing, purifying, renewing, healing.
- Water reminds us of the Source of Life—God and Spirit—therefore, Creation and creativity, or birth of ideas.
- Water is associated with fertility and abundance.
- Water reconnects us with that primal watery haven—the mother's womb—in which our incarnated soul found peace and comfort.
- Water is associated with fluidity, movement, unstuckness—the evolution and transformation of the soul and its needs.
- Water is associated with feminine energy (yin)—God in the Mother and Goddess form.
- Water quenches thirst, thus our desire for meaning in life.
- Water's stillness and reflectivity mirrors the natural contemplative nature of the soul.
- Water gives us fond memories and reconnects us with the inner child, and its sense of awe and wonder and celebration of life.

THE SACRED FOUNT OF SPIRIT

Sacred waters have long held the attention of cultures throughout history. It is somewhat difficult to say why some waters are sacred and others are not. I would like to suggest that the sacred quality of water is directly proportional to the intensity or purity of our human relationship to it. A well, spring, or fountain is made holy, therefore, by the reverential devotion we give to it and its surroundings. And, if we choose to associate this water with our connection to the Divine, then so much more empowered is the natural psychic or electrical energy contained in its location, as scientists and mystics have shown. In short, the Spirit of the Place is nurtured as much by our repeated visits and stewardship as it is by our thirsting for God and Truth.

Ancient traditions have long associated holy wells and springs as very special places of the Goddess or *anima mundi:* symbolic of the Great Mother and associated with birth, the feminine principle, the universal womb, the *prima materia,* the waters of fertility and refreshment and the fountain of life. These *dreaming sites,* as they are called, have also been associated with visions, healing, and other paranormal experiences. In ancient Greece, for example, there were more than three-hundred medical centers placed at water sources, where patients experienced healing.

Admittedly, this is not the type of information you could expect to read on a bottle of Evian or the label that comes with your garden hose, concrete fountain, or pond liner. But remember, we are imagining here that our culture honors the sacred dimension of water. Therefore, we accept that the overarching *feminine* principle of water and its life-giving and healing properties are vital to our survival.

It is one thing to talk about sacred waters in long-established sacred places. It is quite another to suggest that our Sanctuary Garden may itself hold a symbolic key that unlocks the spiritual properties of water in a simple pond, water bowl, fountain, or birdbath. However, part of the development of a gardening theology is to recognize those psychological dimensions as well. And here, we have the keen insights of psychoanalyst Carl Jung into the relationship between garden and water.

Jung made it his life's work to understand the human connection to Nature and the unconscious mind through symbols. He saw the garden, for example, as a symbol of earthly and heavenly paradise and of the cosmic order. Indeed, the ancient Persian gardens mirrored this religious symbolism. The typical Persian garden was divided into two crossed axes. The resulting quadrants symbolized the belief that the universe is divided by the four great rivers of life. In the Middle East, one of those four rivers was the Euphrates, which, together with the Tigris, bordered the famed Fertile Crescent, or what has been called the "cradle of Western civilization." In such walled desert oases, plantings were laid out in neat geometric rows, symbolizing order, and were surrounded by elaborate water features such as canals, fountains, and fish ponds. The history of gardens over the centuries repeatedly demonstrates our human intent to create outdoor enclosures that have order—certainly a mirror of that order we would like to have in our own life.

Jung goes on to suggest that when walled with a small opening to enter, as with a gate, a garden is a symbol of obstacles, hardships and ignorance which a human must overcome in order to attain a higher divine level of consciousness or awareness. And what might you guess symbolizes that active force within the soul—what might be called the collective unconscious—from which one hopes to attain this wisdom or oneness with God? Yes, water.

As an unformed, undifferentiated mass, water symbolizes the abundance of possibilities which precede form and creation. It is the first matter from which life springs. Be it spiritual fertility or fertility of the soil, water sustains, regenerates, and cleanses life, both body and soul.

The form water takes in a garden itself identifies the degree to which one can hold constant in one's efforts toward self-realization (Jung would call this *differentiation*). Water gushing forth, as from a fountain or spring symbolizes the life force that permeates all life—what Chinese metaphysics call *chi* and Hindu spiritualism calls *prana*. This spiritual energy accounts for our individuality and soul urge. Jung suggests that the recycling of water, as in a pond or fountain, is like a circular sea with no outlet. When sitting still, the water is static, as would be the soul in contemplation of truth. But, when it is activated, the recycling nature of water is perpetually replenishing itself, allegorically connecting human to God through the process of soul evolution and transformation.

I find all this symbolism fascinating, if only for one reason: for much of my life I have had a paradoxical relationship to water—on one hand, fearful of it (I twice nearly drowned) and, on the other hand, feeling more than blessed by its presence. It has only been by embracing water in our Sanctuary Garden that I have been able to surrender fully to its spiritual and psychological qualities.

My first notion of the healing and cleansing powers of water occurred as a result of a traumatic divorce. For weeks, I would stand in the shower several times a day crying fitfully over my loss, while my tears converged with first the warm and then the cold spray, as the available supply of water diminished. We each have stories, I am sure, about feeling soulfully cleansed by water, whether it be soaking in a warm bath by candlelight and music, relaxing in a hot tub after a stressful day's work, sitting at the ocean, or even just swimming laps in a dreamlike state. I never forgot the haven of my showers and for a long time afterwards imagined the warm enfoldment of water as being that ethereal state of peace in the womb of my mother. In this sense, Jung's symbolism is correct.

The cleansing, healing properties of water along with its subtle power for fertile rediscovery of passion within the soul are what I attempted to convey in the first water features at Cortesia.

When you come close to our arched entrance, which reads *Spirit and Nature Dancing Together,* you begin to hear the magnetic call of water. It is both intriguing and comforting. Whether you are aware of it or not, you are a pilgrim who has journeyed far and wide to find haven within an oasis of peace. Your soul thirsts for this tranquillity, both without and within. The sound of water reminds your soul of a long forgotten dream, a lullaby sung to you at night while held safely.

Crossing the entrance threshold, you are now in the elongated outer garden of Cortesia. And, along this corridor of perhaps fifty feet or more, you will encounter water in numerous forms. We planned it this way. Each water feature exists as a pearl on a strand, reminding you over and over of its sacred and symbolic importance to life.

Just inside the entrance there is a shallow bowl of water, partially filled with river stones and seashells, encouraging visitors to dip their fingers in it—it is always kept fresh. This first simple water feature—a bowl—is actually so unpretentious that you are apt to miss it. But at the unconscious level it has served to peel away one worldly layer of cares. Nearby you also notice a quaint, well-aged birdbath. Now, you move closer to the source of the sound of water: a spring bubbling forth at the base of a towering 140-year-old Douglas fir, flowing briefly down into a small pool, and then dropping into another larger and deeper one. The setting is as natural as if you were by a mountain brook. The falling water masks all other sound now, and your soul is left to ponder.

In a world of seeming chaos and meanspiritedness, there is a deep thirst for meaning. In his inspiring book, *Touching Peace,* the esteemed Vietnamese Buddhist and meditation teacher Thich Nhat Hanh, points out: "We all need something to believe in, something that proves to us that life is meaningful." In Buddhist mythology, the term *hungry ghost* is used to describe a wandering soul who is extremely hungry and thirsty but whose throat is too narrow for food or drink to pass through. As Thich Nhat Hanh suggests, hungry ghosts long to be loved but may not have the capacity to receive it. They may long to embrace beauty, peace, and truth, but feel incapable of touching these divine virtues.

We all know what this feels like, living in our woundedness, insecurity, lack of self-esteem, feeling burned out and used up. We have been duped into believing that prosperity is measured by money, objects, and unfulfilled desires. And, the fertility of our ideas and abilities are not of value unless they are able to produce or be part of a production process identified as a job or career. At the end of each day, many of us come to the well of our soul as a broken spirit, dried up and thirsty. As the fifteenth-Century mystic Kabir would say, "I laugh when I hear the fish in the water is thirsty." Indeed, we live in a world of seeming abundance, but our soul at times feels as poor as a beggar.

At some time or other in our life, we must measure our inner sense of prosperity and peace by

our connection to God. The sanctuary we receive at this small pool is the holy well from which our soul can drink. Kabir's mysticism is ripe with water imagery as he asks us to consider the true Source of our spirit. He talks of the soul as a house we should not want always to leave in search of God. Listen closely to the musical sound of the cascading water in this Cortesian pool. Kabir says: "What is the sense of leaving your house?/ Suppose you scrub your ethical skin until it shines, but inside there is no music, then what?"

Our soulful immersion into the waters of sanctuary reconnects us again with our own sense of sacredness—our own sense of Godlikeness. "Rain pours down outside," says Kabir, "and inside I long for the Guest." Within our relationship to God is our true sense of prosperity, our belief in a divine sense of order to our life. Just as the water recycles continuously within this pond, we know that God's love and compassion for all beings regenerates hope, faith, and will. God is the great Guest whom we should invite into our lives, and no easier place is there to do this than in sanctuary. As Kabir would have it, find your passion for life in a reverent and intense devotion to Spirit. This is your fount, your source of vitality.

Something has stirred inside you, regardless of whether you are aware of it. It happens at this little pond where a butterfly flits among bleeding hearts, a hummingbird sips nectar, a dragonfly dips close to the water, a bird splashes in a nearby bowl, a frog bellows out a call to a nearby companion. The aura surrounding this pond and cascade is filled with the negatively charged ions of peace and remembrance. More relaxed now, you are more awake, more attentive to the details of Nature around you and the nature of Spirit within.

Before you enter the formal and larger garden at Cortesia, with its varied rooms, you continue to journey up the path. You pass yet another small watercourse that plunges into a deep pool. You surrender easily now to this display of water—you are fully on the other more spiritual side of life's veil, feeling more and more cleansed of worldly chatter. Next to this pool sits a clay jug, an artful gift from a friend. I purposely sat this urn there as yet another symbol of spirit. Cornucopias or urns were often portrayed in Greco-Roman statues, held by a river god and symbolizing fertility and abundance. Once again, Kabir reminds us of the jug's deeper meaning: "If you want the truth, I will tell you the truth:/Friend, listen: the God whom I love is inside."

In a few more feet you are at the arched entrance to the formal garden. Look to your right. Yet

another water bowl sits on a pedastal at the base of another fir, among sweet woodruff, hostas, and ferns. The silver bowl has a sense of royalty as the still, clear water reflects the forest canopy. Look down into the bowl. Therein lies the meaning of your journey through this outer garden, a symbol for that which must constantly and intuitively guide you in your life. Submerged in the transparent freshness is one large stone sculpted in an all-too-familiar shape—a heart.

THEY WILL COME

At Cortesia, it is not important that you receive or understand all the spiritual symbolism of our garden's features. In one sense, they represent our personal expression of reverence for life and the celebration of our relationship with Nature and God. In another sense, we are merely like children innocently at play with some of Nature's many toys.

An insightful child psychologist once said that if you give a child a hammer, then the whole world becomes a nail. We have repeatedly seen a corollary to this in our garden: *provide it and they will come.* Put up a trellis or arch, and every bird in the area will seem to perch upon it. Provide a bench, and someone or something will arrive to sit on it. Set out a water bowl, and all of Nature will appear to take a dip in it.

Yes, our display of water in our Sanctuary Garden gives us spiritual replenishment, but any

Practical Values of a Water Feature

· Masks ambient sounds—street, traffic, city noise, the hum of a nearby pump, and so on.
· Attracts wildlife that need sustenance and a place to bathe.
· Provides in its sound a musical ambience.
· Softens a rocky landscape.
· Captures natural precipitation from rain, snowmelt, and the like.
· Enhances the drama of a setting.
· Cools and makes air lighter by forming more negatively charged ions.
· Creates a reflecting pool for showcasing nearby flowers, vegetation, natural lighting through overhanging trees, and the sky and clouds.
· Showcases garden art—bowls, urns, fountains, barrels, birdbaths, and so forth.

sacred significance would be lost if the features did not express our sense of service to all the non-human visitors to our garden. I want to now share with you some very practical considerations in creating water features in your outdoor sanctuary.

As with each of the design elements of a Sanctuary Garden, consideration should be given to these three qualities: *Aesthetic Attraction, Soul Attraction,* and *Habitat Attraction.* When you begin considering a water feature, however simple or complex it will be, keep these three qualities in mind. Ask yourself, "Does this look nice, is it in keeping with my intent to honor water in my sanctuary (*Aesthetic Attraction*)? Does this feature move me personally, giving me repeated pleasure and contentment, perhaps inspiration when near it (*Soul Attraction*)? Have I considered the needs of other creatures in creating this water feature, however small they may be (*Habitat Attraction*)?"

There is another consideration with any water feature: The sense of placement, form and function must always feel right to you, the Keeper. It really does not matter what others think, and it is entirely realistic to assume that they will not grasp the spiritual symbolism, if any, of your water features. It is enough that you create and care for a water feature with a full sense of reverence, honor, and celebration, letting its esoteric symbolism, if any, seep into your soul effortlessly. Even beyond spiritual considerations, however, if you simply provide water, remember: It will draw a response. Therefore, even before you create a water feature, sit in your sanctuary and visualize water. Look around you, then stroll through your setting slowly. Envision water's presence and sound, if that dimension is desired. Begin to imagine your water feature's location, the form it will take, and most important, its true sense of purpose or function.

I believe that a Keeper's sense of rightness about water must mirror his or her partnership with Nature. And this can only occur by taking the time to observe and study water in natural settings. This is what I call "reading Nature."

Perhaps my greatest love of water has been for creeks, brooks, streams, and ponds. This is where the intimate secrets and stories among rocks, animals, insects, plants, and Nature spirits are told. Park yourself beside such watery waysides, and simply listen and observe. Someone or something here and there is chatting. A little symphony is being tinkered with by some fledgling Mozart.

Rocks and stones are sculpted by the incessant force of water. Pool bottoms are covered with varying-sized stones, with an occasional projecting boulder. Every nook and crevice seems to be occupied by somebody or something—a plant, underwater creature, a few randomly scattered pebbles. Plants and stones line and overhang the banks. Perhaps a shattered log or the smooth root of a tree or shrub is partially submerged. Even the mottled sun or shade seems to have its well-placed seat for part of the day. In your stillness notice the frenetic life of this watery sanctuary as insects appear to jostle for seats at an outdoor symphony.

When you read Nature as a pond or pool in a natural setting, you become in touch with what I call its *keynote.* This concept of keynote is the vibrational energy surrounding a natural feature that calls others to it. It is, for example, the particular way water sounds when cascading over rock and dropping into a pool; the way or sound of water, splashing as from a fountain.

Bioregions have their own strong keynotes. In the Pacific Northwest, the presence of wind and water are particularly magnetic. The wind through firs stimulates life here just as the wind through pines in the upper Midwest or through aspens in the Rockies. Our rain here in the Cascadia bioregion and the abundant movement of water in rivers and streams churns the life force within humans and wildlife alike.

You cannot read about keynotes or feel their presence by reading gardening books, especially books on creating water features. You must discover their intuitive meaning directly. Otherwise, you are apt to create a water feature that is antiseptic in sound or appearance.

I have listened to the sound of water so much in natural settings that when I hear it unnaturally displayed it is like an orchestra playing out of tune. The worst culprit is plastic. Many people want to have a pond in their yard and opt to purchase a prefabricated, often kidney-shaped, plastic pool. They then purchase a plastic cascading watercourse and pump, set the whole thing up, fill the pond with water, place flagstone around the border, plug in the pump, and stand back to admire their pond. I tread on thin ice here, for who am I to say that this simple feature does not give one great pleasure? But the whole scene is too contrived, inspired by a picture out of a catalog or magazine or a nearby garden. The sound of water hitting plastic is unidentifiable to wildlife as is the sheer blackness of the pool bottom. There is no natural flow and variety—shape, form, texture of rocks, and vegetation—around the border.

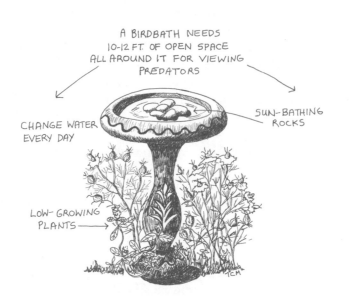

A BIRDBATH NEEDS
10-12 FT. OF OPEN SPACE
ALL AROUND IT FOR VIEWING
PREDATORS

CHANGE WATER
EVERY DAY

SUN-BATHING
ROCKS

LOW-GROWING
PLANTS →

Yes, the ponds and watercourses at Cortesia are constructed using rubber pond liner. But I have developed the features with the full intent of an artist privileged to paint a picture of the Madonna. I want to do justice to the beauty, form, and function of every natural pool I have ever visited. I want to capture that subtle *keynote* that draws life to it. Each rock has been meticulously hand placed, as if the Earth was my canvas, and each rock has often been moved and shifted about to create that natural crook, cranny, or tumbled look. There are dominating boulders of odd shapes intermixed with smooth river rock and small pebbles.

As in Asian gardens, I strive for the right balance between rock, stone, and plant. Japanese gardens are microcosms of the larger drama of Nature. Each part of Nature is represented by a different element. A rock may depict a mountain, the quality of permanence and strength. A flower may represent beauty. Water depicts fluidity, sound, and motion, thereby offsetting the heaviness and immovability of stone. When these features are in proper perspective—and only repeated sojourns into natural settings where water is present will teach you this—then the effect is calming, offering the soul repose and communion with God.

As the Keeper of your Sanctuary Garden, it is your duty to show that you understand at least a few inner workings of Nature that you just cannot read about in a book. Your other obligation is to use common sense. For example, it doesn't make sense to create a wonderful pond, or maybe even set out a whiskey barrel with a little recirculating pump and fountain, and let the plastic liner and tubing, power cord, and submerged pump be exposed to full view. It is okay to be creative in hiding these items. I have routed and hidden tubing beneath rock surrounding the pond, buried it beneath an inch or so of topsoil, even disguised it behind vegetation or with pieces of bark that have peeled off logs. My pond's pump is disguised in the deepest part of the pond (where it should be anyway), either beneath an overhanging rocky ledge or a floating pond plant.

Over and over, you will learn by your errors in thinking, just as I have, and you will develop a discriminating eye and taste in the process: A Sanctuary Garden simply is *different* from any other type of garden. Things that feel out of place or not just right will bug you, and so they should. Even if your sanctuary space is minuscule, here is your opportunity to take just one design feature mentioned in this book and pour your heart and soul into it. If water is an element you want to highlight, become a scholar of water.

Let's take a simple water feature, as case in point—a shallow bowl or basin, such as one would use for a birdbath. Before you even consider such an item, may I suggest you find a little spot somewhere in Nature. It doesn't matter if it's in a park, an empty lot, among highrises, or, preferably, just in wild Nature. Now, look only for sitting water: a rock, slightly hollowed out; an indentation on the sidewalk; a low spot in the grass; a calm, shallow eddy in a stream. After a summer rain is a good time to go to water school. Pull up your seat (not too close) and observe.

A bird swings in and proceeds to splash and preen itself. It would not do this if the pool of water was too deep. A butterfly flutters down to take a sip and comes to rest on an exposed rock to sun itself. It would not partake in its water and sunning ritual if no rock were present. A water skitter

darts across the surface tension of the still, shallow pool searching for tiny insects. It could not do this in moving water. A seed floats down from the sky and pierces the watery surface—food for someone, maybe an attempt to beat the odds and set root in questionable terrain. Even the stillness of the water itself gives you a cinematic treat, mirroring the shapes and textures of passing clouds overhead.

These scenes and behaviors all have something in common: They depict the *drama* that is Nature occurring over and over in countless places for which we humans have little or no regard. Each bit actor is playing out a script encoded in their genetic makeup. Water was provided in just the right form, in just the right place, to serve a purpose.

This is a powerful lesson that I encourage you to take into your soul as your Sanctuary Garden's Keeper. If you create a water feature, try to understand just how it is going to serve the needs of your garden's guests, large and small. Yes, select for yourself a lovely birdbath or ceramic water bowl. This appeals to your sense of aesthetics, and that is important. Find a rock weathered and hollowed by water erosion that will hold small pools of mineral-rich rainwater. Create a turbulent cascading watercourse, if that is your desire. After all, water is a great mask for ambient city noise. In every instance, however, tinker with and adjust your feature so as to allow those gypsies of

Nature who fly, crawl, and walk into your garden to feel right at home. Find your water feature's *keynote* and do this by taking time to read Nature's drama. In time you will begin to read the nature of your soul—what experiences and desires, friendships and interests resonate, like keynotes, within the drama of your life.

It is late in the afternoon now, as I begin to finish these thoughts, and it has just begun to rain. For most of the day, I have been watching the clouds gather and close ranks like an entering gospel choir. Earlier I noticed the wind had shifted and picked up. The towering firs began their familiar swaying dance, and the leaves of various plants in the garden began their curious wiggle. The birds have taken shelter in the woods. Only one soul remains in the garden—Tricia. I admire her passion for gardening. She is as much a piece of art among the garden as any plant or structure, and I know that she will receive the soaking of the rain as yet another baptism of God's love.

I have seen this summer drama played out for years now at Cortesia. It is as familiar as an old pair of summer sandals. So, it is worth saying that one of the most exhilarating experiences of water in your Sanctuary Garden is rain.

Find a simple way to honor rain and dew. Arrange an exposed or sheltered sitting spot out-doors (if it is not too cold) and give yourself a kinesthetic treat. If this is not possible, just sit next to a window looking out into your garden. Running, flowing, dripping, tapping, slapping, patter-ing, and spattering. Create ways and opportunities for rain to find a welcome home in your Sanc-tuary Garden. As your garden's Keeper, demonstrate that you have found a way to celebrate this most readily accessible water feature, truly a gift from the heavens.

In my closing thoughts about water, I cannot help but think that it is really my inner child that is most in awe of this vital life force. Water makes me feel more playful and comforted. Even during winter, when water takes the form of snow and creates amazing features in the garden as it sticks to and balances on trellises and limbs—even then, do I feel wrapped in childlike awe. Deep inside me I pine to capture that innocence of youth, as much so as I want to know that I am wor-thy of the wisdom of my forty-nine years. Water is one way I can lure my inner child back into my life—into the sanctuary of my soul.

As the rain now pelts the roof, our daughter, Sonji, sits a few feet from me, wanting to feel the comfort of her father. I ask her to write a poem about water. I thought she might better be able to articulate the value of water in a Sanctuary Garden. May I offer the view of a twelve-year-old, her whole life lived at play in the gardens at Cortesia.

> Birds warble.
> Bees bumble.
> And all the creatures are stirring,
> except the clear blue waters of the garden.

The Sanctuary Garden

The birds clean themselves in the mystical water,
While the bees suck the sweet nectar
 from the loving flowers.
The wind rustles through the trees,
And the clouds quarrel with the sun.

But the water in the garden
is always the forgiving one.

TIPS FOR USEFUL WATER FEATURES

Shallow Water Bowls

· If used as both garden art and for symbolic display of water, find one that is unique and makes a statement. Let it reflect your values and sense of aestheticness.
· Place bowls on stumps, rocks, pedestals, or on the earth near vegetation.
· Place various sizes of stones in the bowl and make sure one or two are only partially submerged. These are important perches and sunning spots for butterflies, bees, insects, and some birds.
· Freshen the water regularly—this maintains its aesthetic appearance and is well-received by wildlife.

Hollowed Rocks and Indented Surfaces

· Natural catch basins make wonderful and natural-looking water features. Always be on the lookout for such objects.
· Place catch basins and rocks on edges of ponds, paths, or flower beds.
· When dry from lack of rain, simply fill with a hose or water bottle.

Bird Baths

· Carefully select one that, in its color, size and design, feels right and accentuates other features and color schemes in your garden. Let it be artful and functional.
· Try to avoid plastic birdbaths unless they can be generously disguised by surrounding foliage and groundcover.

Water

- Freshen water regularly. Concrete baths will tend to develop algae. Beware of commercial algae removers whose chemicals may be toxic to wildlife. Once a year simply scrub bath with bleach and rinse *thoroughly.*
- Place a few partially submerged stones in bath for wildlife other than birds to enjoy, especially butterflies.
- Locate your bath enough in the open and path of a flyway. Birds are cautious and need to feel that escape from predators is possible from all directions.
- Definitely locate a sitting area nearby for your enjoyment.
- A bath is nice near a feeder. Consider having sandy soil near the bath. Birds use this for two reasons—as a scrubber for preening and to swallow small pebbles that aid in grinding food and digestion in the stomach.
- Some baths (ceramic especially) may need to be stored during winter freezes, lest they crack.

Bogs and Wetlands

- These types of water features take careful planning, based upon observation in natural settings. However, they are exquisite habitat for specimen plants and wildlife, including butterflies, dragonflies and other insects, frogs, and certain birds.
- Because of their specialness, preparation and maintainance (bogs cannot ever dry out), consult a specialist on the subject or refer to a good book.

Fountains

- A fountain is a powerful focal point in a Sanctuary Garden. The right size and degree of ornateness is most important to consider. *Be highly selective.* Most fountains are either too cutesy (molded racoons, birds, angels, bears, or other little creatures clinging to the base or situated atop the basin) or too Romanesque, often depicting a virgin, goddess, or angel pouring forth water as from an urn. Such a fountain may suddenly appear out of place unless it has been purposely selected to integrate with your Sanctuary Garden design.
- Shop carefully for quality and sturdiness—you get what you pay for.
- Plan for a nearby electrical outlet (outdoor approved) to plug in the pump. Make sure to hide any electrical cords. Clean pump once a year, at least.
- Fountains (especially concrete ones) can build up algae over time. Chemical algae removers are available as additives to the recirculating water, but may be toxic to wildlife.
- Always have a seat nearby to enjoy this feature.

· Especially, create a floral display nearby to attract visitors and to accentuate the drama of the setting.

Pools, Ponds, and Watercourses

· The single most important tip is to spend time in Nature where such natural features exist. Observe and listen to the drama.
· Let size and design fit with location.
· Hide and disguise all plastic components, electrical cords, pumps, and so forth.
· If mortaring rocks together as part of the feature, disguise any concrete look by coloring the mix with natural rock tones. (By the way, concrete ponds are highly problematic to consider.)
· Strive for as natural a look as possible—use native rock from your region, create contrast with sizes and textures of rocks, integrate woody surfaces (logs, branches, etc.) that show age, decay, moss, and the like, and plant vegetation that encroaches and fills in niches. Make the edges and embankment varied in appearance. Have rocks in bottom and partially submerged, as with a prominent boulder.
· "Tune" your pond's watercourse or waterfall by arranging and re-arranging rocks and woody debris until the cascading sound feels natural (plastic splashes have a very noticeable slapping and hollow sound). You will be amazed at the numerous auditory effects you can create.
· If you desire fish habitat, use a pond liner or material approved for fish use. Plant vegetation, water snails, and so on that will aid in the pond's cleanliness, beauty, and oxygen supply. Create coves and ledges for fish to hide in.
· If using halves of whiskey barrels or similar large water basins for a small elevated pond, a common planting is water lilies. Research their care and upkeep well. Plant around such an elevated feature to disguise its stark presence. If it has a small fountain, hide the cords, tubing, and pump.
· Specially designed and artful water spouts (as in Japanese bamboo water features) can enhance the attention, but make sure these features naturally integrate with the overall theme and drama of your water feature.
· Plan for regular maintainence of a pond—cleaning fallen debris, pump, water, and so on.
· As always, place a sitting feature nearby.

5

Color and Lighting

Behind the soulfulness of pure, saturated light and color,

as best seen in the myriad flowered faces of Nature,

is the beautiful face of God smiling down

in blessing upon us.

—NARANA

*T*he aspects of color and lighting, taken individually and in their relationships to each other, are very important in the Sanctuary Garden. As with the other design elements of a Sanctuary Garden, one of the primary purposes of color and lighting is to evoke a mood. Thus, you will want to pay close attention to the connection between light and color and to the effect that various colors and color combinations have on your moods and emotions.

While color has long been important in many cultures because of its powerful effect on the body, mind, and spirit, the use of color in gardens has only come into primary focus in more recent times. There were ornamental gardens, history tells us, in ancient Egypt, China, Japan, Greece, and in the Roman Empire. But, in Europe, the first gardens were created at convents and monasteries with a very practical intent in mind. In fact, the patron saint of gardening, St. Fiacre, was a prince-turned-monk in the Middle Ages, whose monastery in Breuil, France, became a mecca for people who came to be healed by the medicinal plants he grew there.

Such monastic gardens were primarily used for the cultivation of herbs and, for reasons of efficiency, designed very symmetrically with rows of neat, straight beds. This rather unnatural layout continued for quite a long time, even in the ornamental gardens of the Renaissance and Baroque periods. The plants, in this latter case, were less important than the formal design, which was often dominated by carefully pruned hedges, meticulous pathways, and elaborate topiary shrubs. There was still no conscious use of color.

In England, finally, in the early eighteenth century, there began a trend toward a more natural type of garden design, where the focus was more on the plants. By now, there was also an increasing diversity of plant material to choose from, because of the influence of the popular botanical gardens and new varieties being brought back and propagated by travelling horticulturalists.

Another shift was occuring as well—a growing interest in the use of color in the landscape. This movement was influenced significantly by the English landscape designer Gertrude Jekyll. In her book *Colour in the Flower Garden* (now called *Colour Schemes for the Flower Garden*), first published in 1908, Gertrude drew extensively on her training in art and color theory to create richly contrasting color combinations and stunning visual effects. Modeste Herwig, in *Colorful Gardens,* observes that Gertrude "painted with the colors of plants," making her the first "impressionist gardener." Gertrude Jekyll laid an admirable foundation for a subsequent exploration of the art of gardening with colors, which continues to this day. The British are now famous for their lovely and exuberant cottage gardens and their magnificent perennial borders, based purely on the colors and textures of plants.

In France, Impressionist painter Claude Monet made his own mark on this evolution of thinking. Beginning in 1883, in his garden at Giverny, he became fascinated with the effect of light on colors, a key relationship in the Sanctuary Garden. Monet discovered that the garden's colors appeared different in the cool light of morning then they did in the bright, warm light of the midday sun. He explored these differences extensively in the many beautiful paintings he created, often in his own lovely garden, which has now been restored and opened to the public. Like Jekyll and Monet, whether creating a mood of melancholy or joy, mystery or romance, one must first be able to deeply feel that mood in their own heart and soul. Then it can take physical form in one's garden.

COLOR-FILLED *Ragas* OF FRIENDSHIP

When seen in a historic/cultural context, yet filtered through our own deep sense of intuition, the careful consideration and use of these elements can yield rich results. History offers us many examples of the worship of the sun, for instance, and we may choose to draw on the richness of some of these images, stories, and characters to understand color and lighting. By doing so, we re-experience the archetypal fascination with light and all that it symbolizes in human consciousness.

From the ancient cultures of Babylon, Sumeria, Egypt, and Assyria to the great empires of the Incas, Mayans, and Aztecs, from Europe to the far East and beyond, the beauty and power of the sunlight was honored and celebrated. In Phoenicia, Baal, god of the burning sun, was referred to as a god of health. His son, Gibil, was the noon sun god who protected people from the plague. In Egypt, although the pharaoh himself was regarded as a god, each morning, after being purified by the priests, he climbed the stair to the great window to salute "his other self, the sun."

Hindus worshipped the morning sun deified as Vivasat. And they composed beautiful musical pieces, called *ragas,* to be played at very specific times of the day to capture the essence and soul of that time. There were peaceful dawn *ragas,* energetic noon *ragas,* plaintive or soulful evening *ragas,* and so on, each with its own special rhythm and mood. Each raga shimmers with its own unique quality of light and aliveness, as if transporting the listener to a series of gardens to experience the passing of the day and the changing light amongst the flowers.

In our Sanctuary Gardens, we would do well to create color and plant ragas that praise and capture a certain mood or time of day based upon its lighting, or glorify a particular color or even a person that we dearly love. In reflecting upon how I might have done this, I realize that in many ways it is my dearest friends in life whose energy and presence reside in the various plantings in our gardens. And, so, my garden is really a series of plant ragas composed for the colorful characters who have so much influenced our lives.

My dear friend Harriet lived at "Peace Place," a "garden with a house in the middle of it," as she was fond of describing it. She was a poet and writer, a peace activist/networker, an expert in the art of solar cooking, a wonderful chef, a devoted meditator, and natural gardener (among other things). Harriet nearly always wore white. It was part of her spiritual tradition, representing the peace and purity of the soul. When she died tragically in India two years ago, I missed her terribly; and a month or two later I began wearing white for the first time in my life. It has had a powerful effect on me. I've also begun planting more white and silver-leaved flowers in the garden. And, if that's not enough, the medicinal herb, feverfew, has been coming up everywhere in my beds with an unusual double white flower that a well-known herbalist calls the most beautiful feverfew she's ever seen. It positively glows, especially on darker days, in the evening, or in the moonlight.

What is it about wearing white or gazing into the upturned face of a lovely white flower? Why have I never cared for the color white before? I suppose I saw white as being the absence of color, although it actually contains all the hues in the spectrum. And it just wasn't bright enough or interesting enough for me. I found it boring and, of course, impractical to wear. But now, I feel a sense of peace and tranquility when I am around white. It allows my mind to rest somehow, to come to stillness. And, perhaps, as it has throughout history, white represents to me a type of purity of thought and action, heart and soul.

In losing Harriet, who was one of the best models of peaceful thinking and being that I have ever known, I have had to draw more deeply from my own reservoir of peace and pure-heartedness. Because I feel so much more grounded these days and in touch with the accessibility of sanctuary, I know that our garden and our entire property emanates a much stronger vibration of peace than it ever has before. It's not that we are saints, of course. But the effort to think and act peacefully day by day, year by year, seems to accumulate in a place over time. I am certain of this. You may experience a similar evolution in consciousness, and you can be sure that every creature and every plant around you will breathe in your peace and soak in your joy. That is the sacred and symbiotic relationship that becomes so apparent in a Sanctuary Garden.

Our Favorite Whites at Cortesia

Astranti (*Astrantia major*)

Bugbane/Black Snakeroot (*Cimicifuga simplex or racemosa*)

Candytuft (perennial) (*Iberis*)

Christmas Rose (*Helleborus niger*)

Clematis (*Clematis—armandii, recta purpurea*)

Echinacea (*Echinacea "White Swan"*)

English Daisy (*Bellis perennis*)

Feverfew (*Chrysanthemum parthenium*)

Foamflower (*Tiarella cordifolia*)

Lily-of-the-Valley (*Convallaria majalis*)

Love-in-a-Mist (*Nigella damascena*)

Mullein (*Verbascum alba*)

Obedience (*Physostegia virginiana*)

Oriental Lily (*Lilium orientale "Casa Blanca"*)

Rockcress (*Arabis caucasica "Snowcap"*)

Rogersia (*Rogersia pinnata "Alba"*)

Sandwort (*Arenaria*))

Shasta Daisy (*Chrysanthemum maximum*)

Sweet Woodruff (*Galium doratum*)

Yarrow (*Achillen millefolium*)

Yucca (varieties) (*Yucca*)

Shrubs

Mock Orange (*Philadelphus lewisii*)

Ocean Spray (*Holodiscus discolor*)

Slender Deutzia (*Deutzia rosea campanulata*)

Viburnum (*Viburnum—davidii & doublefile*)

Barbara, on the other hand, is a healer, and she has found her sense of playfulness and celebration of life. She loves hot pinks and purples. A dutiful and devoted nurse, wife, and mother for years, I met her shortly before her youngest child went off to college. She was entering, as was I, a period of deepening spiritual exploration.

We learned the wonderful technique of *Usui Reiki* at the same time in the early '80s, and little did we realize back then what an important role *Reiki* (meaning "universal life energy" in Japanese) would play in healing the inevitable wounds of our past and leading us into our healing work with others. *Reiki* uses gentle touch to move energy through the body and remove blockages, pain, and tension. I have done so much *Reiki* that now its energy is always present in my hands regardless of what I'm doing. Whether I'm gardening, holding one of our cats, touching someone, whatever, I feel a kind of tingling aliveness in my palms and fingertips.

Clearly, *Reiki* has been Barbara's touchstone, too, and I have seen how this alignment with her life's service has freed enormous amounts of stuck energy, resulting, in Barbara's case, in a real zest for life. I think that's why she loves bright colors. Not only does she wear lots of hot pink and purple but she uses the same colors in her garden. Among her favorites (and now mine) are the perennial asters, the intensely fragrant stargazer lilies, lavender, purple lobelia, lilacs, and any dahlia with pink in it. Looking around our garden, you can see Barbara's exuberant influence. Not only has she shared with me the sacred *Reiki* healing techniques, but most recently she's convinced me of the mystical qualities of the iris, a vigorous flower I have long avoided. In fact, on a recent trip to the famous Schreiner's Iris Gardens south of Portland, Oregon, she ordered us three hundred dollars worth of iris bulbs. Okay, so now one of my most weed-ridden beds is being turned into a premier iris bed. Bless you, Barbara, for the raga of joyful purpose and healing you have given to our sanctuary.

Enter my wonderful friend Morgan, formerly an impeccable, high-energy businesswoman and motivational seminar leader across the country, and mother of five. I met Morgan about two years after she had been stricken with a mysterious, toxic poisoning from a new housing project where she worked. It nearly killed her, leaving her bedridden and helpless for over a year but because of her great courage, Morgan has allowed herself to become transformed. To heal one's physical body and at once forge a spiritual link that demands a certain nonattachment to physical pain and emotional suffering is a great challenge. And I am learning along with her. (I shattered my hip on Mt. Rainier while backpacking with my son. I had a long period of physical immobility followed by gradual rehabilitation. This was during the same time as Morgan's illness, though we didn't know each other yet.) We have chosen to try to slow the pace of our formerly frantic lifestyles that we may have time to ponder life's deeper mysteries and enjoy some of life's simple pleasures.

Morgan's home, which she shares with her devoted husband Robert, is a true sanctuary. It is a haven for birds and squirrels and other wildlife, but also a haven for humans. Inside, the walls are painted in the softest golden color, warm and enfolding, bright yet peaceful. Soothing earth tones abound in every room, as they do in the clothing Morgan wears so elegantly. "I used to wear bright colors," she shared with me, "but not anymore. I am no longer trying to get the world's attention. My journey is more inward now, which seems to call for quieter colors."

This comment has influenced me a lot. I'm wearing more earth tones myself lately (when I'm not wearing white) and have a greater appreciation for the softer, more subdued hues in clothing, artwork, and plants. I've also tried to capture in our garden something of the golden quality I find so pleasing in Morgan's home. So far I have only found a few plants that even approximate it: the lime-mound spirea, the golden form of lamb's ear, golden feverfew, the lovely corydalis lutea, and the pale yellow flowers of moonbeam coreopsis and phlomis samia. Perhaps that golden hue is best experienced as the late afternoon raga of the sun low in the sky, casting long shadows and bathing everything in a warm glow. This is a raga of releasing the distractions in our day and coming back into a focus on spirit. Thank you, Morgan, for that.

A final guiding influence I wish to share has come to me through one of my oldest and dearest friends, Terra. Being a tall woman of inner and outer strength, she has an appreciation for plants of substance—tall and bright. She particularly loves dahlias and ornamental grasses, and we enjoy growing and sharing special varieties we think the other will like. Being sincerely devoted to meditation, Terra has a deep sense of what sanctuary is about. When she first sat in the Meditation Garden, in an early stage of its development, she intuitively felt the need for more privacy there.

Within a week after her visit, Forrest built the fir branch fence that now separates the Meditation Garden from the rest of the garden.

Through her loving friendship over all these years, Terra has provided for me an enduring sense of sanctuary, and she has responded appreciatively to each stage of the creation of our Sanctuary Garden. Hers is the raga of loyalty and devotion to friendship and to the Divine Spirit that shines through all beings, be they human, plant, or animal. In honor of her "light of friendship," I have planted bright dahlias in the Meditation Garden.

So, you see, my friends are like the flowers in my Sanctuary Garden. If you spent time at Cortesia, perhaps

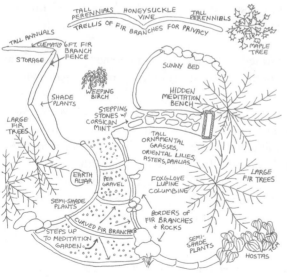

LAYOUT FOR MEDITATION GARDEN

you would begin to hear, as I do on some inner plane, the many ragas that comprise the multicolored musical tapestry of my soul and the soul of our garden. Each of you has your own stories to tell and friendships to honor and, as these memories take physical form in your garden, you will be amazed at what solace you receive from them. Many seemingly separate strands of your psyche and your life experiences will become woven together in the most beautiful garden tapestry, unique in all the world. You may even discover or rediscover parts of yourself little known or long forgotten. As Harriet wrote in her unpublished manuscript, *The Inner Garden,* "The garden is like that—always teaching, always showing simply by its presence the next lesson I am ready to learn about it and about myself."

LETTING THE SOUL SPEAK THROUGH COLOR

When we are intuitively attracted to a certain color or lighting condition for reasons we cannot entirely articulate, it is really our soul rising up. The beauty of a Sanctuary Garden is indeed this more soulful awareness of the language and artistry of Nature, speaking to us through plants, animals, rocks, wood, water, and myriad other forms. Spoken language cannot describe the range of feelings and insights we may have when in a state of spiritual sanctuary. Yet we might all agree that we *do* need better words to more clearly describe the subtle nuances of colors and their mutations in various light conditions. More than that, however, we need to develop a deeper awareness of Nature's incredible artistry. And, we need to seek a clearer understanding of God's purpose and intention behind placing Nature's colors so conspicuously all around us.

As the Keeper of our garden and soul, we might each do well to learn the language of color and lighting—to be the Keeper of Color and Light in our place of refuge. I like what Diane Ackerman has to say about the language of color in her book, *A Natural History of the Senses:*

"The color language of English truly stumbles when it comes to life's processes. We need to follow the example of the Maori of New Zealand, who have many words for red—all the reds that surge and pale as fruits and flowers develop, as blood flows and dries. We need to boost our range of greens to describe the almost squash-yellow green of late winter grasses, the achingly florescent green of the leaves of high summer, and all the whims of chlorophyll in between. We need words for the many colors of clouds, surging from pearly pink during a calm sunset over the ocean to the electric gray green of tornadoes. We need to rejuvenate our brown words for all the complexions of bark (and soil). And we need cooperative words to help refine colors, which change when they're hit by glare, rinsed with artificial light, saturated with pure pigment, or gently bathed in moonlight."

Color speaks to us in ways that are at once therapeutic, healing, and spiritually deepening. These qualities are not only for our own human benefit, but they also serve to enhance or deepen the psychic power or energy of a natural setting. For example, the ancient Chinese practice of *Feng*

Shui (literally translated as "wind and water"), focuses on the art of placement, balancing and enhancing the environment. *Feng Shui* makes very concious use of color, and even recommends where to place objects of a particular color in relationship to the entrance or other energy centers of one's home or garden.

Rather than using a formal technique, such as *Feng Shui,* you might choose to go about making your plant and color selections very intuitively, based on how you "read" or "hear" the energy and drama of your setting. For example, while we love bright colors here at Cortesia, we have clearly chosen more of the softer hues to promote a gentle, soothing effect. Shades of pink, white, lavender, and purple predominate, with a few blues, pale yellows, and lots of silver. The more intense colors like orange, red, and royal blue are used sparingly as occasional accents and focal points, or to create stronger contrast or special interest. These stronger colors are also necessary to ground the energy of the garden and to parallel the incredible drama provided by towering 150-foot trees surrounding the main garden.

I am personally intrigued by the healing properties of color, as demonstrated in color therapy, and in the spiritual dimensions of color as seen in our body's seven energy centers or *chakras.* Taken together, these two languages of color have valuable application in the Sanctuary Garden and in the healing of both body and soul.

The body's seven *chakras* are power centers located from the base of the spine to the top of the head and that correspond to the seven major colors: red, orange, yellow, green, blue, indigo,

Seven Useful Tips on Color and Lighting

· **Lead with your heart.** Reflect on the mood and feelings you want to capture in your special place of refuge. Consider those ways you want to celebrate Nature, friendships, memories, and so on.

· **Keep it simple at first.** Initially, select only a few colors (2–3) in a given area. Dabble with Nature's canvas, integrating plants, wood, rock, and the like. Learn from these initial experiments and explore new ideas in other locations.

· **Sit and observe.** Place sitting features near your handiwork to determine if you've achieved the effect you desired. Visit this spot at different times of the day, noting the subtle, yet often powerful, effect of lighting on your color and textural choice of plants. This lighting will help validate the effects you are attempting to create.

and violet. Each *chakra* absorbs a special current of vital energy through its particular color ray. These colors are taken in through the physical environment and from higher levels of consciousness.

The color ray that each *chakra* attracts is necessary to the rainbowlike harmony of the whole person. In the use of color healing, the individual's aura around their body is actually studied to see where gaps in this rainbow aura might exist. Any condition of disharmony, whether physical, mental, emotional, or spiritual, implies the presence of either an overabundance or an inadequate supply of a particular color vibration.

Color healing would then be undertaken via ingestion of vegetables and fruits of that color. Or one could drink special water that had been steeped in the sun for several hours in an appropriately colored glass bottle. Color visualizations or fifteen-minute treatments under a color lamp might also be recommended, using the appropriate color filter. Interestingly enough, in the literature on chromotherapy, I have seen no mention of the therapeutic value of growing flowers of the desired color nor the idea of simply spending time in proximity to them, but we don't need a healer to tell us that.

You probably already know intuitively what colors you like the best, as well as those you are least attracted to—but have you ever wondered why? You may learn something about yourself by studying the *chakra*/color associations. I know I did. Furthermore, in your garden you can experiment with adding more of the colors that represent qualities or influences you want to increase in

· **Know flowering times of plants.** Remember to match the flowering times of plants in a given area so your color combinations will not be wasted. However, consider planning for sequential flowering throughout the gardening season, letting different colors arise or blossom to subtly evoke a different mood.

· **Think about light.** The quality of light is important to plant growth and vitality. Know what your plants need. Furthermore, observe throughout the day how lighting affects the colors and foliage of plants as well as the textures of leaves and bark.

· **Plan for compatibility.** Be sure that the textures and color of leaves and foliage is considered in your design—you will most likely be seeing the leaves of your favorite plants much longer than the flowers themselves.

· **Know plant maturity characteristics.** Plants mature at different heights and widths. Some plants have greater leaf spread than others. Plan so that taller or more vigorous plants don't smother shorter or more delicate ones.

yourself. For example, while I love best the cooler colors from green up to violet and white, and use a lot of these colors in the garden as a means to strengthen my inward spiritual focus, I appreciate the occasional burst of yellow, orange, or red (when well placed) to infuse me with vital energy and celebration of life. Let me now share with you some insights I have gained to the therapeutic and spiritual value of colors in the design of a Sanctuary Garden.

THE EXUBERANCE OF RED

Red is warm, vigorous, and energizing. Author and color master Modeste Herwig says it was the first real color (besides black and white) to be named in nearly every language. Red can be linked with aggression, war, blood, and lust. However, this rather masculine color, when used carefully, can represent or stimulate passionate love, activity, courage, and movement. In *Feng Shui,* red, when properly placed enhances fame and relates to wealth and also harmony in marriage. In color therapy, red-orange is a very enlivening color that is said to increase blood pressure, speed up breathing, and enhance poor circulation. A red or orange light is reported to be good for sore muscles and sore throats and stimulating to the growth of plants.

Too much red can make a small garden seem even smaller. Also, in the Sanctuary Garden, which is often designed for peace and quiet, an overabundance of red can be too exciting and energizing. However, red may be just the color you want more of if you suffer from depression, lethargy, or a general lack of motivation. Experiment and see for yourself.

Once, when our daughter Sonji was in a serious bicycle accident, I gave her a red columbine to hold during the long drive to the emergency room—red for courage, I told her. As the doctor began putting stitches in her knee, Sonji then decided to visualize a deep blue sky and a peaceful blue ocean. She was amazingly calm throughout her ordeal. Author Amrit Pavani calls this the "Rainbow Prayer," where we literally immerse ourselves in a chosen color and deeply experience its healing qualities. What better place to do this regularly than in our Sanctuary Garden.

You may want to soften or diffuse some of the intensity of red in your garden by surrounding it with purples, whites, pale pink, silvery plants, or dark green or burgundy foliage. Then again, you might choose the option of actually brightening the red effect even more by juxtaposing it with other warm colors such as orange or yellow. In a popular gardening magazine, I recently read with delight an article by a woman who has finally accepted the fact that her entire garden is planted with red and yellow flowers. In spite of all the disapproving comments made by her refined gardening friends, she refuses to budge from her strong preference for these two colors.

Among the perennials with red flowers are many varieties of roses, tulips, dahlias, rhododendrons, and those listed in the "Our Favorite Red Plants" chart. In annuals, verbena, geranium, and impatiens are good (if not overused) long-blooming choices. I also love the vivid red of *Crocosmia lucifera,* the delicately beautiful leaves of the woodland ground cover *Epimedium rubra* (green

Our Favorite Reds and Pinks at Cortesia

REDS

Bee Balm (*Monarda "Cambridge Scarlet"*)

Cape Fuchsia (*Phygelius copensis [Coccineus]*)

Cardinal Flower (*Lobelia cardinalis*)

Columbine (N.W. native) (*Aquilegia formosa*)

Japanese Blood Grass (*Imperata cylindrica*)

Maltese Cross (*Lychnis chalcedonica*)

Monbretia (*Crocosmia "Lucifera"*)

Pineapple Sage (*Salvia elegans*)

Sedum (*Sedum spectabile*)

Sweet William (*Dianthus barbatus*)

Trees & Shrubs:

English Holly (red berries) (*Ilex quifolium*)

Heavenly Bamboo (*Nandina*)

Japanese Maple (*Acer Japonicum*) fall color

PINK/ROSE

African Daisy (*Osteospermum*)

Annual Mallow (*Lavatera*)

Annual Candytuft (*Iberis cruciferae*)

Bleeding Heart (*Dicentra*)

Clematis (*Clematis montana "Rubens"*)

Coral Bells (*Heuchera*)

Common Aubretia (*Aubretia*)

Cranesbill (varieties) (*Geranium*, perennial)

False Spirea (*Astilbe*)

Farewell to Spring (*Clarkia elegans/Godetia*)

Filipendula (*Filipendula*)

Foxglove (*Digitalis*)

Japanese Anemone (*Anemone hybrida*)

Kaffir Lily (*Schizostylis coccinea*)

Lenten Rose (*Helleborus orientalis*)

Love Lies Bleeding (*Amaranthus caudatus*) annual

Nicotiana (*Nicotiana solanaceae*)

Oriental Lily (*Lilium orientale "Stargazer"*)

Phlox (*Phlox subulata*)

Red Valerian (*Centranthus ruber*)

Sedum (*Sedum telephium "Autumn Joy"*)

Thrift (*Armeria*)

Twinspur (*Diascia*)

Winter Daphne (*Daphne odora*)

Trees & Shrubs:

Crabapple (*Malus*)

Peony (*Paeonia*)

Rhododendron   (*Rhododendron*)

tinged with red), the red/bronze autumn fern, and the deep red in some of the newer *coleus culti-vars.* Keep in mind that in the reds we include many nuances of that color, from deep red or burgundy to a fire engine red, from orange-red to a rosy red. In your explorations you can determine for yourself exactly which shades, if any, are most pleasing to you. In any case, remember that red's exuberance in your garden is uplifting to the soul, making you happy to be alive.

THE VITALITY OF ORANGE

In color therapy, orange, like red, has a positive, energizing, and encouraging effect. Similar to yellow, it stimulates the nerves and is the color representing warmth, willpower, radiance, and vitality. In Nature, orange is closely associated with autumn because of the turning of the leaves and the ripening of certain berries at that time of the year. In small doses, orange can be very refreshing, but it can also become overpowering. Walking up the plant-lined sidewalk to our friends Robert and Penelope's house the other night, we were visually embraced by a small but positively glowing patch of bright orange nasturtiums. Forrest and I were both stopped in our tracks by the lifting effect. Keep in mind that the effect was successful, at least for us, because it wasn't overdone.

Orange looks lovely and cheerful with reds and yellows, and also against green or silvery foliage. I happen to love orange with deep burgundy or with blue and indigo (like in our sunset bed). And it can be quite stunning when mixed with white (more white than orange).

Perhaps the key to integrating the color orange into the Sanctuary Garden is to recognize that we all need orange power in our lives to some degree. The dynamic qualities connected with it are part of any balanced personality. Even the most confident individual will no doubt experience days or periods when they are discouraged. To be able to wander out into the garden at such a time and stand or sit next to the nearest orange flower could be just the cure the doctor would never dream of ordering.

The unspoken symbolism of orange represents a vitality and will that cannot be beaten down. For example, during my "orange period" in my twenties, I finished college, left my home state and family, found my passion in photography and nature, survived a serious car accident, and endured the death of my mate. Oftentimes, I would bear the weight of an oversized orange backpack and escape into the high Rockies for days, where my emotional emptiness was gradually filled with new hope and aliveness. The color orange itself hasn't changed my life, but undoubtedly I am drawn to it when needing the willpower and energy to overcome my fears and limitations. Sit me down in front of a glowing campfire or a beautiful sunset and I instantly remember who I am and what I hope to accomplish in life.

Our Favorite Oranges at Cortesia

Cinquefoil (*Potentilla nepalensis* "Miss Willmott")
California Poppy (*Eschscholzia californica*)
Chinese Lantern (*Physalis alkekengi*)
Coneflower (*Rubideckia fulgida or hirta*)
Daylily (*Hemerocallis*)
Monbretia (*Crocosmia*)
Nasturtium (*Nasturtium*)
New Zealand Flax (*Phormium* "Rainbow Warrior")

Pot Marigold (*Calendula officinalis*)
Oriental Poppy (*Papaver orientale*)
Red Hot Poker (*Knipphofia*) orange/peach
Rose (*Rosa* "Joseph's Coat") climber
Siberian Wallflower (*Cherianthus allionii*)
Spurge (*Euphorbia* "Fireglow")
Trollius (*Trollius* "Prichard's Giant")
Tulip (*Tulipa* "Apricot Beauty")

Trees & Shrubs:

Catoneaster (*Catoneaster*) orange berries
Flowering Quince (*Chaenomeles*)
Japanese Maple (*Acer Palmatum*) fall color
Mountain Ash (*Sorbus*) fall color, berries

Paperbark Maple (*Acer Griseum*) orange bark
Persimmon Tree (*Diospyros*) orange fruit
Staghorn Sumac (*Rhusthyphina*) fall color
Sweet Gum (*Liquidambar*) fall color

THE WISDOM OF YELLOW

Yellow, the color of the sun, is bright and cheerful, and, like orange, is warm and stimulating. It brings to mind, of course, that characteristic radiance of the sun, the luminous, yellow-green leaf shoots of spring, and the early bloomers such as daffodils, forsythia, crocus, and primrose. What a welcome and uplifting sight those first spring flowers are, as are the summer favorites such as goldenrod, coneflower, sunflower, and the ever-popular marigold.

Yellow, being the brightest color, is linked symbolically to knowledge and clear thinking. In the Far East it is the color of wisdom, even holiness. In paintings of the Old Masters, yellow, or the noble color, gold, was associated with the hereafter or the heavenly light, as in the halos of saints. Ironically, in *Feng Shui,* yellow relates to the Earth and also supports children. In tenth-century China, according to Modeste Herwig, yellow was reserved exclusively for use by the Imperial Court. In contrast to the Asian symbolism, beginning in the Middle Ages, Europeans considered the color a sign of treason, because it was associated with bile. It was also linked to envy, hatred and betrayal.

In color therapy, however, the preference for this color denotes a creative, enthusiastic person

Our Favorite Yellows at Cortesia

Alyssum (*Alyssum mentanum* "Gold Dust")

Angel's Trumpet* (*Brugmansia*)

Common Yarrow (*Achillea millefolium*)

Common Mullein (*Verbascum thapsus*)

Coreopsis* (*Coreopsis* "Moon Shine")

Coreopsis (gold-burgundy) (*Coreopsis* "Zagreb," "Tinctoria")

Corydalis (*Corydalis lutea*)

Curry Plant (*Helichrysum angustifolium*)

Cotton Lavender (*Santolina chamaecyparissus*)

Daffodil (*Narcissus*)

Dandelion (*Taraxacum officinale*)

Day Lily (*Hemerocallis* "Stella D'oro," etc.)

Evening Primrose* (*Oenothera*)

Fried Eggs (*Limnanthes*)

Golden Lamb's Ears (leaf)* (*Stachys*)

Japanese Forest Grass* (*Hakonechloa macra aureola*)

Jerusalem Sage* (*Phlomis fruticosa*)

Kahili Ginger* (not hardy) (*Hedychium gardneranum*)

Lady Mantle (yel.-green) (*Alchemilla mollis*)

Lupine (*Lupinus* "Chandelier")

Ligularia (*Ligularia dentata* or *przewalski*)

Mullein* (hybrids) (*Verbascum*)

Red Hot Poker (*Kniphofia* "Little Maid," "Citrina")

Sunflower (*Helianthus*)

Violet* (*Viola cornuta*)

Yarrow* (*Achillea* "Moonshine")

Thyme (yel./green leaf) (*Thymus* "Doone Valley")

Trees & Shrubs

Cinquefoil (*Potentilla fruticosa*)

Deodor Cedar (golden) (*Cedrus deodara*)

Forsythia (*Forsythia*)

Golden Chain Tree (*Laburnum*)

Japanese Aucuba (*Aucuba japonica*)

* = light yellow

who can be somewhat aggressive as well. Yellow is very stimulating to the nerves and brain, and has been shown to have a harmonizing effect. I know it does for me.

In the Sanctuary Garden, yellow is a happy color that is bright without being overwhelming or intrusive. It will enliven a small, dark, shady area, making it seem more cheerful and expansive. Golden-leaved or gold/green variegated plants, such as those mentioned in Chapter 3, also have the same effect. They provide a glowing contrast to the medium greens of most foliage or the darker greens of the conifers.

I am also particularly fond of the pale yellow flowers. They feel more subtle and gentle than the bright yellows, and at times they are almost etheric. Pale yellow blends quite well with a variety of other colors—and don't forget the pastoral quality of yellow dandelions and the good-natured English daisies with their golden centers. Why kill off these harmless beauties with pesticides and herbicides? We receive so many appreciative comments from visitors who enjoy our natural lawn.

It makes them feel relaxed and at ease, and it saves us a lot of time. Most of us seem to work too hard in our gardens anyway, doing things we don't need to do. Better to spend the time sitting and enjoying all the work Mother Nature does free of charge.

THE HEALING POWER OF GREEN

Over eight-hundred years ago, in the turbulence and creativity of medieval Germany, there lived an extraordinary woman by the name of Hildegard von Bingen. The youngest of the ten children of a German knight serving the castle of Bickelheim, Hildegard had visionary experiences even as a child. From the age of eight, she was raised and educated in a Benedictine monastery, where she took her vows when she was eighteen. In 1136, at the age of thirty-eight, Hildegard was appointed abbess of this monastery, and four years later began having her celebrated series of visions, called the "Illuminations." She painted these visions in the form of mandalas and wrote extensively about them over a ten-year period in her first book, *Scivias* (Know the Ways).

One of the most wonderful concepts that Hildegard gifts us with is a term not used by any other theologian: *viriditas,* or "greening power." She speaks eloquently about "the exquisite greening of trees and grasses," of "earth's lush greening." She writes that all of creation and especially humanity is "showered with green refreshment, the vitality to bear fruit."

Hildegard draws an intimate connection between creativity and greening power, stating that "greening love hastens to the aid of all. With the passion of heavenly yearning, people who breathe this dew produce rich fruit." It is a fruit that remains, a fullness that does not wither. In the words of theologian Mathew Fox, author of the book *Illuminations of Hildegard of Bingen, viriditas* is "God's freshness that humans receive in their spiritual and physical life forces. It is the power of springtime, a germinating force, a fruitfulness that comes from God and permeates all creation. This powerful life force is found in the non-human as well as the human."

Today perhaps we relate to the color green more simply as the predominant hue of Nature. In *Colour Healing,* author Mary Anderson links green to balance, peace, and harmony. It brings "a feeling of renewal, of new life, freshness and brightness, rather like the coming of spring." That says it for me. How often have we each gone for a drive in the country or had a picnic in the park just so that we could be in the healing presence of so much green?

To most of us, a world without green is unimaginable, but it may well be that in our Sanctuary Garden the most important (and taken for granted) color really is green. Therefore we may want to pay particular attention to our selection of just the right trees and shrubs and leafy plants, over and beyond whatever fruit or flower color they might possess. It's important to me to love all stages of a plant's growth, and not just wait impatiently for the blooms. *Viriditas* calls forth from our soul an unconditional love for all of Nature in every season. It offers us a deep sense of solace any time of the day and all year long.

A Few of Our Favorite Greens at Cortesia

Greenish Flowers

Lady's Mantle (*Alchemilla mollis*)

Hellebore (*Helleborus foetidius*)

Spurge (*Euphorbia*)

Ferns

Autumn Fern (*Dryopteris erythrosora*)

Holly Fern (*Cyrotomium*)

Japanese Painted Fern (*Athyrium goeringianum* "Pictum")

Licorice Fern (*Polypodium glycyrrhiza*)

Royal Fern (*Osmunda*)

Sword Fern (*Polystichum munitum*)

Western Maiden Hair Fern (*Adiantum pedatum*)

Large-Leaf Plants

Bear's Breech   (*Acanthus mollis*) showy flowers

Gunnera (*Gunnera tinctoria*)

Hosta (varieties) (*Hosta*)

Ligularia (*Ligularia*) yellow-orange flowers

Ornamental Artichoke (*Cardoon*) silvery green

Rogersia (*Rogersia*) white plumes

Silver Sage (*Salvia argentea*) white flowers

Sword Fern (*Polystichum munitum*)

Ornamental Grasses

Blue Fescue (*Festuca cinerea*)

Flame Grass (*Miscanthus sinensis* "Purpurascens")

Fountain Grass (*Pennisetum alopecuroides* "Hameln")

Golden Variegated Hakone (*Hakonechloa macra* "Pureola")

Japanese Blood Grass (*Imperata* "Red Baron")

Northern Sea Oats (*Chasmanthium latifolium*)

Silver Banner Grass (*Miscanthus sacchariflorus*)

Skyracer Moor Grass (*Molinia caerulea* "Skyracer")

Tall Switchgrass (*Panicum virgatum* "Strictum")

Variegated Japanese Silver Grass (*Miscanthus sinensis variegatus*)

Variegated Purple Moor Grass (*Molina caerulea* "Variegata")

Yellow Sedge (*Carex elata* "Bowles Golden")

Zebragrass   (*Miscanthus sinensis* "Zebrinus")

The healing color of green is really the cornerstone of the Sanctuary Garden. This is less by our choice, in all actuality, than by Divine decree. I imagine that there are easily more shades of green than any other color, and with good reason, considering that green is the color of the heart chakra. Perhaps it is meant to help protect us from the effects of heart disease or console us in the case of a broken or lonely heart.

So, drink in the green if you are so fortunate to be able to do so. Surround yourself as best you can with the heart-soothing shades of what I believe must be God's favorite color. Why else would there be so much of it? If green is indeed the color of hope, peace, and healing, could we ever experience too much of it? I think not. Even as green serves as the bridge between the cool colors of the spectrum and the warm colors, it symbolizes the connection between the vitality of our physical body and the quietude of our soul, via the heart. In *Feng Shui,* green is important in the realms or *ba-guas* of knowledge, wealth, and family.

If by chance you take the green world for granted or tire of it in your garden, learn to explore the many shapes, textures, and shades of green. You may discover a rich world awaiting you. Consider contrasting large-leaf plants with more delicate ones, smooth or round leaves with heavily veined or very elongated leaves. Juxtapose, if you like, the yellow-greens, the blue-greens, and/or the gray-greens. Let the bright green of a large-leaf hosta, for example, play off the deeper green and more delicate leaf of the fern, beneath the still-darker green of conifers. Contrast airy clumps of ornamental grasses with lush ground covers like baby tears, corsican mint, or wooly thyme. Or underplant the dramatic gray green spikes of kniphofia with the low-growing golden oregano. The possibilities are endless.

BLUE AND INDIGO: DOORWAYS TO SPIRIT

One of the most vivid memories I have from my childhood is of sitting by the kitchen window while my mother cooked dinner. I would gaze raptly out at what she poetically calls "the blue hour," that waning light of day after sunset. Our yard was filled with huge oaks, elms, and maples, but in winter the quality of the Blue Hour was heightened, because the sky was more visible through the bare trees. Their powerful black silhouettes were glorious against the deepening sea of luminous blue.

I have been profoundly affected by my childhood experience of the Blue Hour and its subsequent influence on my understanding of color and its love affair with light. But what is it about that time of day that is so sacred? Why do I feel called away by the Blue Hour from

VIEW FROM THE SUNSET BENCH AT CORTESIA

whatever work I am doing, however important it may seem to be? Like so many others, I have a strong tendency to keep myself very busy throughout the day. But, as evening approaches, some ancient biological clock silently sounds within me calling me back to God.

In *A Natural History of the Senses,* author Diane Ackerman speaks about craving "the visual opium of the sunset." But sunset and the Blue Hour were created, I believe, to be so very beautiful precisely so that they would entice us to leave our worldly concerns far behind. This is not to numb us, but so that we might contemplate the wonder and beauty and deeper meaning of life. I do this automatically each evening as soon as I walk out of the "sunset gate," a Japanese-style arched gate that leads from the garden out into the deep woods that sweeps down our dramatic ridgeline.

In the past, I often worked in the garden until it was too dark to see. Now I usually stop willingly that I might rest my weary body and turn inward. Evening, I believe, is a time of prayer, affirmation, and gratitude for the lessons and blessings of the day. "Each day accept everything that happens to you as coming directly from God," the great Indian sage Paramahansa Yogananda once said, "and each night give it all back into His hands." That is what I do in the Blue Hour: I willingly release the day and return it to God.

Sitting there on the sunset bench or on my favorite mossy log perched at the uppermost edge of the ridge, I gaze out across lush green valleys and forestland to layer upon layer of distant hills. I am one with all beings, and at peace with myself. I have no more expectations of the day, no more agendas, no further plans. I become the philosopher, the sage (or *saga,* as wise women were once called). Whatever life experiences rise up to the surface of my consciousness, I filter through the calm realization that they have been a gift in some way to the evolution of my soul. Judgements, worries, fears, are magically lifted as if by some unseen hand. God seems very close and accessible during the Blue Hour, and the craziness of the world seems ever so far away.

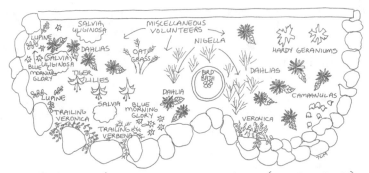

THE EVER-EVOLVING "SUNSET BED" IN BLUE, PURPLE, & ORANGES (5×13' W/ ROCK BORDER)

Color and Lighting

Just a little while ago, I watched again, as if for the first time, the beauty of the last traces of orange-coral clouds retire into the deep, deep blue of night. And, suddenly, I understood why for two years I have had the overwhelming urge to plant a flower bed all in shades of violet-blues and oranges. From time to time, certain colors seem to rise up in us, do they not, begging for expression in our lives. While orange and blue isn't a color combination I'd likely wear, in Nature any and all colors seem to fit together admirably. Certainly these two colors are as compatible as any. Long inspired by the transition of sunset into the Blue Hour, I wanted to create what I call a *sunset bed*.

My work on this project actually began when I totally dismantled an existing wooden raised bed and moved all the remaining plants. Then I hauled many large basalt rocks from our neighbor's sheep pasture, tossing them over their fence, and wheelbarreling them down through the woods and into the garden via the sunset gate. (No doubt some of the rocks I uncovered had not seen the light of day for thousands of years, if ever. Think about that.)

In any case, after I constructed the rock bed, I added lots of compost and some fertilizer to the

Our Favorite Blues at Cortesia

African Lily* (*Agapanthus*)

Amethyst Flower (annual) (*Browallia*)

Blue Ginger (not hardy) (*Dichorisandra thyrsiflora*)

Blue Star Creeper (*Laurentia fluvaiatilis*)

Borage (*Borago officinalis*)

Chinese Forget-Me-Not (*Cynoglossum amabile*)

Cornflower* (*Centaurea cyanus*)

Delphinium (*Delphinium* "Blue Fountains," "Giant Pacific")

Desert Bluebells* (*Phacelia campanularia*)

Dwarf Plumbago (*Ceratostigma plumbaginoides*)

Forget-me-not (*Myosotis alpestris*)

Gentian Sage (*Salvia patens*)

Herb-of-Grace (*Rutagraveolens*) blue-green leaf

Larkspur* (annual) (*Consolida*) (*Delphinium ajacis*)

Larger Forget-me-not (*Brunnera macrophylla*)

Lithodora (*Lithospermum diffusum*)

Lobelia (annual) (*Lobelia*) many shades

Love-in-a-mist (*Nigella*)

Lungwort* (*Pulmonaria*)

Monkshood* (*Aconitum*)

Perennial Geranium (*Geranium* "Johnson's Blue")

Speedwell* (*Veronica*)

Squill (*Scillia amethystina*)

Windflower (*Anemone blanda*)

Shrubs

Blue Hydrangea* (*Hydrangea*)

Wild Lilac (*Ceonothus*)

* = purple-blue

clay soil and planted the blue and blue-violet flowers. There were perennial *salvia uglinosa,* tiny trailing veronica, stately native lupine, dainty nigella, and perennial verbena and campanula ground covers. I was uncertain about the oranges so I planted pinks, mostly cosmos and dahlias. It didn't work. The blues felt right but the pinks did not. Ironically, none of the pink flowers survived the ensuing wettest winter in Oregon history, so now I have added the orange flowers: California poppies, several shades of lovely orange and coral dahlias, and tiger lilies.

I've been reformulating this little vision for months now, letting it live and grow in me even as the sunset does night after night. Like a rich and fragrant medicinal tea, the idea has required ample time to steep and deepen to its full potency. Now I am ready to let the dream come to life. And what was once merely a flitting butterfly of my imagination will soon have an articulated form that may, in turn, inspire others who come here seeking sanctuary. Perhaps when my mother next visits our garden, she will in some way receive a small measure of the peace she helped me to appreciate when, so many years ago, she introduced me to the Blue Hour.

Blue, being the color of the sky, is a symbol of infinity and the heavens. It is generally associated with calmness, sincerity, and honesty ("true blue"). People who prefer blue, from a color-therapy standpoint, are said to be "meticulous, stable, and satisfied with what they have achieved." But too much blue can be inhibiting, passive, and even a cause of depression ("the blues") and fatigue for some. In *Feng Shui,* blue, like green, is used especially to stimulate success in the areas of knowledge, family, and wealth.

Interestingly enough, there aren't many blue flowers. I've learned that what is often called blue may actually be blue-violet or bluish-purple. Plants in this range are restful to the eye and can make the garden look bigger. They are particularly lovely in a Sanctuary Garden, we feel, especially when contrasted with a color such as white, pink, orange, purple, or even pale yellow. You do have plenty of choices because almost any color can look good with blue and will enliven it if they are not too similar.

The blue *chakra* itself is the doorway to the spirit. Therefore, in general, blue will have a restful and calming effect in your Sanctuary Garden and lend a sense of spaciousness. Place it anywhere you want these effects. I've also seen blue ceramic planters or water bowls or even deeper-blue garden chairs used very effectively if not overdone.

VIOLET/PURPLE:
ROYAL NATURE OF THE SOUL

Purple is considered the darkest of the main colors. It may not show well in the garden unless it is surrounded by lighter or brighter colors, such as white, pink, pale yellow, or even orange or red. Violet, of course, being paler than purple, shows up quite nicely unless it is placed near pink. When shown to their best advantage, flowers in the violet/purple spectrum can be very impressive.

Our Favorite Purples at Cortesia

Acanthus (purple & white) (*Acanthus mollis*)

Aster (*Aster*)

Beard Tongue (*Penstemon* "Sour Grapes")

Bellflower (Peach-leafed, Dalmation, Tussock,
   Harebell) (*Campanula—persicifolia, portenschlagiana,
   carpatica, rotundifolia*)

Carpet Bugle (variegated) (*Ajuga* "Burgundy Glow")

Catmint (*Nepeta mussinii*)

Clary Sage* (*Salvia sclarea*)

Clematis (*Clematis* "Jackmani," etc.)

Clustered Bellflower (*Campanula glomerata*)

Columbine (varieties) (*Aquilegia*)

Common Sage (*Salvia officinalis*)

Dahlia* (varieties) (*Dahlia*)

Delphinium* (varieties) (*Delphinium*)

Gayfeather* (*Liatris*)

Germander (*Teucrium lucidum*)

Hollyhock (varieties) (*Alcea rosea*)

Hyssop (*Hyssopus officinalis*)

Jacob's Ladder* (*Polemonium*)

Larkspur (annual) (*Delphinium*)

Lavender (Spanish, French, English) (*Lavandula—
   stoechas, dentata, augustifolia*)

Lilac* (*Syringa*)

Ligularia (purple leaf) (*Ligularia* "Desdemona")

Loose Strife (*Lythrum* "Fire Candle")

Meadow Rue* (*Thalictrum*)

Mexican Bush Sage (*Salvia leucantha*)

Money Plant (*Lunaria annua*)

Morning Glory (dwarf) (*Convolvulus tricolor*)

Obedient Plant* (*Physostegia virginiana*)

Pansy (varieties) (*Viola*)

Passion Vine (*Passiflora*)

Purple Coneflower (*Echinacea purpurea*)

Rose* (varieties) (*Rosa* "Angel Face," etc.)

Sedum (mauve) (*Sedum* "Autumn Joy")

Self-heal (*Prunella*)

Summer Phlox* (*Phlox paniculata or subulata*)

Tree Mallow* (*Lavatera*)

Wallflower* (*Erysimum* "Bowles Mauve")

Shrubs

Butterfly Bush (*Buddleia*)

Rosemary (*Rosemary officinalis*)

Smoke Tree (leaf & flower) (*Cotinus coggygria*
   "Royal Purple")

* = violet

They possess at once the excitement of red and the peacefulness of blue. Since red is considered masculine and blue feminine, purple is said to be the color of love, being a blend of red and blue. It is also mysterious and is linked to the unconscious.

In deep meditation, focusing on the third eye (the point between the eyebrows) eventually reveals a violet color that is profoundly peaceful. Although color therapy links the preference for

Lighting in Cortesia

HANNA YOSHIMURA, ARTIST

I knew Tricia and Forrest for several years before I felt ready to ask to paint at Cortesia. The first time I visited Cortesia was the summer of 1996. I drove through the Cortesia Sanctuary gate, down through the woods to a light green meadow and their house. Next to the house was another gate made from branches with a sign atop it reading "Spirit & Nature Dancing Together."

Tricia guided me through the wooded outer garden to an arch, beyond which I could see the bright light on a summer garden. It was like opening a treasure box. The plants were shining like jewelry. I will not forget this first impression of the Cortesia Sanctuary.

I painted all that first summer at Cortesia. Now I am in my second full summer, painting for this book. I feel as Claude Monet must have felt. When I look at the garden with impressionist's eyes two things attract me.

The first attraction I describe as, "The sunlight seems to be dancing in the Cortesia Sanctuary." This is because it is located near the top of a hill, so it is close to the sky or heaven. The air is clear. When the sun reaches the garden, everything reflects the forest and the sky, even small stones. The green leaves and flowers cannot be painted with plain pigment. They are radiant in their coloration. I can only *try* to express my feelings about them.

The second attraction of the gardens at Cortesia Sanctuary is what I describe as, "The light seems to make garden art play hide-and-seek." For example, in shade, objects are sometimes influenced by sunlight then hidden again in different degrees of shade. I can only *wish* to paint these changing moments themselves. I offer this poem to describe my experience.

purple to lightheartedness, cheerfulness, and interest in the unusual, I know of many people (including myself) who feel differently. We are drawn to purple as a symbol of Spirit, contemplation, and even royalty. Hence, it is a wonderful color for a Sanctuary Garden.

Two of my favorite combinations are purple with silver-leaf plants (such as echinacea and artemesia) and combinations of violet, blue, and purple. (Delphiniums offer the full range, from the lightest blue to the deepest purple). In the latter case, be sure to mix some lighter shades with

July 15,
The Morning in Cortesia

10:20 A.M.
The sunlight is still gentle
morning breeze playing with the windchimes
and through the Cortesia garden
I am sitting in the wisteria arbor
This is my studio today

10:30 A.M.
The sunlight is starting to bathe the Narana Stone
She seems to be taking a shower in the sunlight
Near by yellow flowers turn into gold
lighter colored leaves turn into silver
mauve flowers turn into sapphire
bees come,
pale pink flowers turn into ruby
hummingbirds come,
I do not need a watch
I will start my paintings with a sundial
My brush stops on my palette
to paint the Narana Stone

the deeper ones for optimal effect. These colors give a sense of restful spaciousness, and seem to stimulate the opening of the heart on a more noble or spiritual level. Excepting white, purple seems to be the color we use the most here at Cortesia. I never get tired of it.

It takes time and devotion to learn the language of color and lighting in the garden. Your tastes are sure to change over time, reflecting your inner evolution. Seeing the garden as a canvas for your celebration of Nature's palette is a wonderful expression of the soul's love of beauty and artistry. Your own inner intuition, however, is often your best teacher, but don't forget that Mother Nature will always have a few surprises up Her sleeve as well. Perhaps your greatest insight will be that this glorious exploration of light and color and their interrelationship is really meant to illumine the many facets of your being and personality. No one else can really speak for the needs of your heart and soul, so don't limit yourself. Know that as you think just a bit more consciously about the meanings certain colors seem to have for you in your life and how you actually feel in proximity to them, you will come away with a greater understanding of your true soul nature.

6

Sitting

If you feel spiritually empty, visit a winter garden cloaked in barrenness.

Underfoot is hope stirring, alive, warming itself without expectation.

The fallen fruit has melded with the compassion of Earth.

In your soul, too, is a season called grace, and therein lies

the seed of a new spring, where life has a chance to blossom

again. It is okay to sit on the garden bench and pray

with such realization, for your emptiness has led

your footsteps to such a holy sanctuary,

to such a sacred place in time.

—MIASHA

There is great comfort in not feeling compelled to go into the garden *to garden*. Imagine just sitting still—very still—whether amidst or on the fringe of the garden. Surrender to the power of the garden—become an appreciating patron. I do this all the time. One day, for example, I sat very still in the garden while Tricia went about her planting rituals. I watched a lone butterfly dip low to Tricia's head, then flutter from flower to flower and to the wings of an ornamental angel and, finally, with great glory, to the palm of my resting hand—all as a matter of course, it seemed, in making the daily rounds to dispense unsolicited blessings. Such moments are why I care for the garden with reverence.

But should we not want to see the garden that is our life in the same way? Not with shoulders drooped and burdened, hands incessantly buried in the duties of the day, eyes and mind fixed on objects and desires, successes and failures, yesterdays and tomorrows. No, not in terms of quiet desperation, but inner devotion should we serve our soul. It is not entirely necessary to *do* in order to *be*. When we give ourself the gift of sacred time in a special place, we are feeding our spirit with love.

Indeed, to sit in sanctuary is to love ourselves anew. It is to allow ourselves to be one with, aware of, and witness to Creation that *is* an act of love. We learn that it is not necessary to act upon Creation to receive this love.

By taking quiet time—in our garden, in our daily life—we surrender our human will to that of the will of Creation. We bear witness to life in this Earth Sanctuary. Unfortunately, many of us miss this opportunity. Instead, we are blinded by a frenetic pace that seems to pick away at our will, character, dignity, and ability to handle stress. Our cities and places of employment seem so much more powerful than we have the will or courage to respond to. Indeed, we need the refuge of stillness, quiet, and solitude. We need some way to regenerate our sense of spirit and hope.

TALL & ARCHING PLANTS AND OVERHANGING FIR TREE
CREATE A SECLUDED EFFECT IN MEDITATION AREA

When we began developing the design concepts of a Sanctuary Garden years ago, Tricia and I knew immediately that the whole idea of taking sanctuary within the garden (or other outdoor settings) *had* to be based upon the act of sitting still, as if we were monks afoot in the world in need of a place for prayer. By quieting the fidgety body and mind in repose, one naturally enters a reflective, observant, meditative state that is essential for the soul. Be it in secretive places in the garden, a special chair or bench on the patio or beneath an arbor or tree, or simply a favorite spot indoors looking out onto Nature—each of these can become an act of devotion to occasional much-needed solitude. In such solitude, we feel a deepening appreciation and gratitude for sacred space and time. We feel more whole again, more in touch with that silent throbbing pulse that is the internal and eternal heartbeat of Creation.

In the gardens of Cortesia there are numerous sitting areas. It is difficult to give patented advice on how you can create sitting features in your own outdoor sanctuary. After all, a seat is a seat, right? Well, yes, if you are merely looking for a device to plop down upon. But what about your soul, your spirit, your guardian angel? What about the Spirit of the garden? What about those visiting spirits of ancestors and mentors and exemplars who still roam the Earth travelling amongst the wind? What about a favorite pet, a passing sparrow, a sunning butterfly, a meandering ant, or even a fallen maple leaf? What I am saying is that your Sanctuary Garden is not just for *your* respite and repose. When you create a sitting spot, make it special, put your heart into its location and design. You don't know who's coming by for tea and blessings.

We believe the best place to start in considering a sitting spot is inside—inside your soul, that is. You should want to *feel* inspired to find solace in your garden. This feeling, Tricia and I believe, is itself generated out of two insights: the need to experience regenerating peace in your daily life, and the need to approach life in such a way that honors and celebrates the sacredness of others.

My dear friend, you need to *sit* in your garden or yard and meditate on the well of inspiration deep inside your soul that moves you into a relationship with Nature. In fact, you need to sit often to reach such clarity. Gardening, as an industry, is devoid of philosophy and spirit. It is up to you to provide this much-needed dimension yourself, for most likely the larger garden that is your life needs to be nurtured by an inner philosophy and spirit as well.

By seeing your yard or garden as a place of refuge—by seeing your own being as a sacred sanctuary—you have the opportunity to create a compassionate sense of self that sees life anew. Saint Paul used the term of "putting on the mind of God," and Brother Lawrence called his personal sense of devotion to reverence "practicing the presence of God." These devotions are purely Cortesian, mirroring the reverential revelations of most native cultures: Seeing each human, flower, tree, rock, insect, animal, sunrise, drop of water as though it were being seen for the first time, and showing courtesy, respect, and honor through overt expressions of artistry, ritual, ceremony, and kindness.

Falling in love with Nature anew awakens us to the fact that She *is* our Beloved, our breathy tether to life, and She *is* the inner child we long to touch in sweet innocence and adoration, not because we are human apart from Nature, but because we *are* Nature, a part of which is human.

In the Sanctuary Garden, and especially so when sitting, we have the opportunity *to be one with, aware of, and witness to* Nature that is humanized for our soulful pleasure, and our own human self that is naturalized for the pleasure of the garden.

Sitting Visualization

Imagine that you are coming home from a hard day at work or perhaps a frantic afternoon of errands and rush-hour traffic. You take deep breaths driving home and eagerly anticipate some regenerative time in your garden sanctuary. You may have even already arranged this with your family—that you have sacred time and space *before* you have to start dinner. As you pull into your driveway, you already know exactly where you'll sit. You greet your family briefly with hugs and gratefully head out to your favorite bench. The path to it is well worn and comfortingly familiar. You know every plant along the way, but you resist the temptation to weed or deadhead, two of the myriad garden tasks that always seem to steal away your time.

You arrive at the bench with a kind of "beginner's mind." Sitting here you look out upon a scene you've gazed at many times before. Yet it all looks new and fresh to you, as if some little angel or gnome has taken special care to love this spot while you were away. Taking in every visual detail with full attention, you also hear the birds

SITTING WITH THE ESSENCE OF A FLOWER

Hearing Forrest speak about experiencing an inner attunement with Nature, as guided by a Cortesian reverential philosophy, reminds me of my own unfolding awareness with plants, which I want to share. About four years ago, a popular local herbalist offered a class here at our Center entitled "Magical Herbs." I admit to being a little uncomfortable with the subject, as I feared that perhaps she would get too "cosmic," leaving practicality behind. But, in actuality, the class was quite fascinating. Halfway through the day, the instructor led us out into the garden and directed us to stroll among the plants. We were to look for a plant with which we felt a strong connection. Then we were to *sit* on the ground next to it and attune to its particular energy.

I was certainly willing to do this, but I had little expectation of any great revelation. I wandered through the herb garden and eventually approached the raised vegetable beds. Near a succulent bed of lettuce and carrots, I caught sight of a tall clump of golden yarrow. I sat down beside it and closed my eyes. Without any effort or thought, I suddenly realized that this yarrow had a very strong presence. Indeed, it seemed to be wordlessly communicating to me an understanding of its essential nature.

singing for the first time today (no doubt you've been too busy to notice them). You smell the fragrant blooms of several plants you purposely placed near the bench for precious moments such as this. As you slowly close your eyes, their intoxicating scents and colors blend in your mind's eye like a beautiful impressionist painting. You glow with a warm light that seems to shine from within.

The gentle breeze and the soft light of early evening wash over you as you sit in stillness. Little by little, the stresses and obligations of the day easily slip away. In these timeless moments, you feel deeply in touch with the part of yourself that is peaceful, calm, and loving. You can forgive all the little injustices dealt you by a world that has now receded, placing you out of reach, inviolate. You drink in the solitude, not even caring about the neighbor kids playing noisily next door or the droning sound of a lawn mower across the street. These distractions cannot touch you. On this bench, in this place of refuge, you have learned that you can experience sanctuary any time you need it. You resolve that you will come here even more often. Your soul whispers, "Peace be with you. Carry my love in your heart."

So clear was this experience that I found it quite impossible to question its validity. I knew that this plant served as an exemplar of tremendous stamina and a kind of inner power and strength that radiated out across the garden, uplifting the other plants. Don't ask me how I knew this, but I did.

When the group reconvened, I shared my experience with surprising confidence. The others easily accepted that this felt right. At the end of the day, when everyone had gone home, I eagerly returned to the garden with a single purpose in mind—to determine if I could in fact "read" any other plants besides the golden yarrow. I visited and sat with my favorite dahlia, a clump of fragrant lavender, a lovely blue-flowering borage plant, and a vibrant golden calendula. Once again I felt a strong sense of the essential nature of each of the plants. I could see that each variety had a personality, just like humans do, with subtle variations in plants within a species.

One simply never knows what knowledge lies hidden deep within one's psyche and soul, but taking the time to sit and nurture these unfolding insights has been the key for me. Who can tell when some deep truth, long-buried within us, is finally ready to emerge? Like an ancient and sacred rock in the earth, it simply awaits our conscious awareness to bring it into the welcoming light of day. Yet if we seldom slow down long enough to perceive these truths, we may never know what precious gift has been lost or simply not properly cultivated. "Solitude is the price of great-

ness," the Indian master Paramahansa Yogananda once said. I have come to know that this is true. So, how do you envision finding refuge by sitting in your special outdoor setting? Here are some practical suggestions.

PLANNING YOUR SITTING AREA

In her quaint little book, *The Garden Bench,* Mirabel Osler reminds us: "Sitting in your garden is a feat to be worked at with unflagging determination and singlemindedness . . . Have you ever noticed how few sitting places you find in private gardens? How seldom the versatility and importance of benches is considered? True gardeners, with their peerless taste, dexterity and inspired planting, never stop . . . To sit is almost an offence, a sign of depravity and an outrage towards every felicitous refinement that has gone into making a garden . . . *I* am deeply committed to sitting in the garden."

Tips on Creating a Sitting Area

· Have a clear purpose or intention in mind as you create your sitting area and select a specific type of sitting structure.
· Carefully select foundational plants (trees, shrubs, flowers, etc.) that will create a focal point of interest, and provide year round, or at least three-season interest, for the viewer.
· Layer smaller plants—flowers, grasses, ground covers, and so on—around the focal point(s). Planting such plants may happen long before you select your bench or chairs, for its takes time for a bed to mature.
· Make your sitting area accessible so people will want to sit there!
· Choose or make benches and chairs that are really comfortable and relaxing to sit in.
· Let the view from your sitting area, whether expansive or intimate, be inspiring and free of clutter.
· Let the thoughtful addition of garden art, a water feature, a prominent anchor stone, or a wind chime enhance the mood of your setting.
· If you have more than one sitting area, let each reflect a different mood or purpose. Consider the following functions: meditation and contemplation, a shady private retreat spot, tea and conversation, sunset viewing, outdoor dining, wildlife viewing, flower gazing, taking in the fragrant scent of a favorite plant.
· Whatever type of setting you create, sit there often, letting it become a place saturated with peace and gratitude.

If your garden currently lacks a good sitting area (due to cultural influences or your own high standards of productivity), here are some points to consider. These would also apply to upgrading an existing sitting area.

First of all, it's helpful to have a *specific purpose* in mind. For whom or with what intention are you creating this sitting area? As a place to gather informally with friends or family? As a quiet, secluded spot where you can go to contemplate or be alone? Perhaps you want a shady place in which to retreat from the heat of the sun, or a vantage point from which you can gaze out across your garden, a water feature, or a favorite flower bed. A bench near a fragrant rose bush or honeysuckle may delight your senses. You may even wish to favor a particular time of the day and its associated activity, like a sunset-watching bench facing west. In every instance, consider your sit-

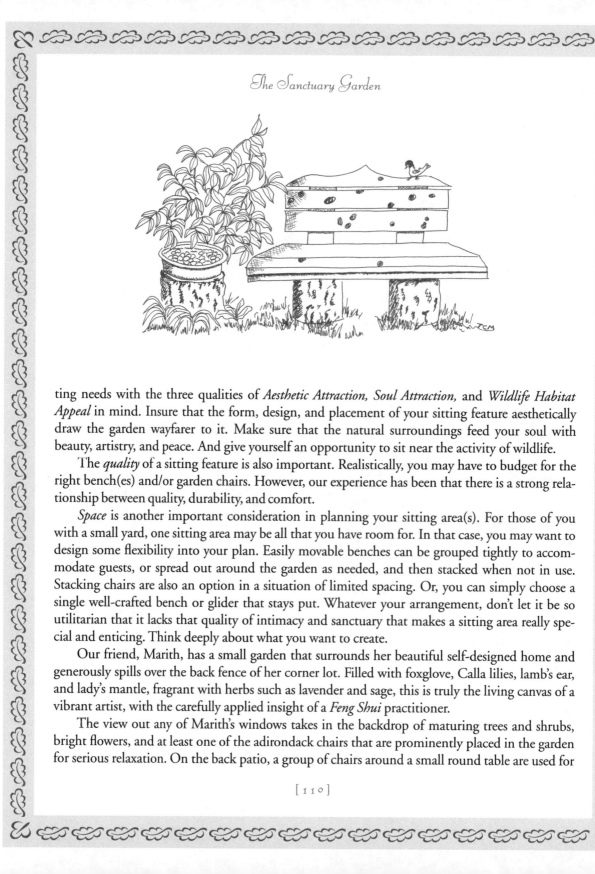

ting needs with the three qualities of *Aesthetic Attraction, Soul Attraction,* and *Wildlife Habitat Appeal* in mind. Insure that the form, design, and placement of your sitting feature aesthetically draw the garden wayfarer to it. Make sure that the natural surroundings feed your soul with beauty, artistry, and peace. And give yourself an opportunity to sit near the activity of wildlife.

The *quality* of a sitting feature is also important. Realistically, you may have to budget for the right bench(es) and/or garden chairs. However, our experience has been that there is a strong relationship between quality, durability, and comfort.

Space is another important consideration in planning your sitting area(s). For those of you with a small yard, one sitting area may be all that you have room for. In that case, you may want to design some flexibility into your plan. Easily movable benches can be grouped tightly to accommodate guests, or spread out around the garden as needed, and then stacked when not in use. Stacking chairs are also an option in a situation of limited spacing. Or, you can simply choose a single well-crafted bench or glider that stays put. Whatever your arrangement, don't let it be so utilitarian that it lacks that quality of intimacy and sanctuary that makes a sitting area really special and enticing. Think deeply about what you want to create.

Our friend, Marith, has a small garden that surrounds her beautiful self-designed home and generously spills over the back fence of her corner lot. Filled with foxglove, Calla lilies, lamb's ear, and lady's mantle, fragrant with herbs such as lavender and sage, this is truly the living canvas of a vibrant artist, with the carefully applied insight of a *Feng Shui* practitioner.

The view out any of Marith's windows takes in the backdrop of maturing trees and shrubs, bright flowers, and at least one of the adirondack chairs that are prominently placed in the garden for serious relaxation. On the back patio, a group of chairs around a small round table are used for

Fifteen Wonderful Reasons and
Places to Sit in Your Refuge

- To be alone in a quiet spot.
- To engage in intimate conversation with another.
- To engage in meditation, contemplation, prayer.
- To view a sunrise, sunset, or sweeping perpsective of the garden.
- To be near children playing in a special play area.
- To be with friends/family in a communal activity area centered around dining, conversation, picnicking.
- To be near the comfort of a favorite pet or animal.
- To be near water and water sounds.
- To listen to the wind through trees, grasses, and windchimes.
- To celebrate the beauty of a particular flower bed or art piece.
- To rest from garden or yard work.
- To take a sun bath in a bright sunny spot.
- To rest in a cool and shady spot on warm days.
- To view wildlife near feeders, nesting boxes, baths, blossoms.
- To simply have a place to do nothing!

tea and conversation, but the other chairs are clearly meant for solitary use, as Marith lives alone. She doesn't sit enough, she confesses, but the reminders to do so are never far away. "I want my garden to be my friend," she says. Undoubtedly, what she means is that she also wants her garden to befriend her.

If limited space is not a concern for you, than you can let your imagination have free rein. You can have a bench for every purpose. It might be interesting for the moment to demonstrate how our friend Liz uses benches and her unique garden settings to provide sitting needs in a variety of ways.

Liz has two chairs at the very front of her garden under the deep shade of a mature conifer. These are conveniently close to one of her main work areas and they also allow a view across to the main entrance. These chairs allow Liz to take short breaks in between weeding and watering, and provide a place to sit and read her mail.

A second sitting area at Liz's sanctuary—her favorite spot—is at the highest point of the garden. Thus, it looks down across her beautiful flower beds. Here she has placed a glider with arms wide enough to accomodate a cup and plate on each side. There are two matching chairs and a table as well. Liz says she loves to drink her morning coffee here while she enjoys the view, or an area like this could be used for sunset viewing.

A third bench is arrived at by way of a secluded little path. It is surrounded by large planters with stunning arrangements of flowers, and backed by speciman shrubs. This has become a good place for solitary reflection among the beautiful, cool, shady plants.

Further back in Liz's garden there is a fourth sitting area—a wrought-iron-and-wood bench with a chair on either side—situated under the shade of many tall oak trees. It is spacious yet intimate. And since it is totally hidden from view by tall shrubs and lush flower beds, it comes as a delightful surprise to the visitor. It also features garden art and a lovely contemplative water basin. This sitting area provides both privacy and serenity.

At the very back of Liz's garden is yet a fifth area with a small bench tucked into a dense thicket of woodland plants. Liz says she works her way back to this spot depending on how noisy the neighborhood children are at the time. She could certainly disappear there, and also be out of earshot of the street traffic as well as the children.

What is really memorable about all these sitting areas is that each one is distinctly different and yet so artfully conceived. One could easily feel inclined to move from area to area—to enjoy a sweeping view, to wishing one brought a good book, to feeling the need to meditate, or to engage in spirited conversation. You see how well one can evoke certain responses based on clear intentions? That is what creating a sanctuary is all about. What can your heart's imagination conceive?

FINAL THOUGHTS ABOUT SITTING

As you can see, a Sanctuary Garden elevates the necessity of solitude or repose to a whole new level in garden design. However, it is up to you in your visioning to create *places* in your garden that can absorb the worldly and human concerns with which we are all burdened. As a couple and family, we are especially aware of the benefits of a special spot where a "peacemaking bench" can be put, where resolution of personal or family issues is the goal. The stronger your perceived need for such a place, the more articulate your vision should be to choose just the right setting, private in one sense but with an inspiring view that fosters inner expansiveness. The deeper your intent, the more powerful will be the healing you receive from conceiving such a place and spending time there.

A Sanctuary Garden, by its very nature, implies an unspoken code of conduct that helps us to process inner or outer upheaval. Whereas it may not be the place to release intense anger or frustration, it *can* be the place to sit and process such feelings. Conflict is an inevitable part of life. At times it can be difficult to come to agreement on even the simplest thing, like the exact placement of a plant or bench or how often to water. We speak to many couples who struggle with these issues. In the face of such controversy, the higher purpose of the sanctuary often rises up and magically asserts itself. Thus it is entirely possible that conflict resolution can then occur in the garden as well, by design.

In fact, Forrest and I must sometimes find sanctuary in our garden *from each other.* One day, for example, I worked for hours in The Shrine part of the garden. I have been sculpting this area, plantwise, for years, using a number of particularly beautiful ornamental grasses born to grow tall, dance with the wind, and flower spectacularly. They are one of the keynotes of our Sanctuary Garden.

So on this particular day, I planted some lovely new varieties: fountain grass, switchgrass, and more blue fescue, with a flowering yucca, a passionflower vine, and a hops vine thrown in for additional interest. After digging and preparing the soil in the heat of the afternoon, I very carefully placed each plant with an eye for balance, future size, and naturalness. Being home alone, I gratefully worked right through dinner. Forrest arrived home near sunset and I excitedly led him up to the shrine to survey my new plantings.

To my great disappointment, however, he had little to say about the enhancements. Instead of praising my artistry or at least appreciating my hard work, he insisted I move the yucca over six inches so that it would not grow and obscure the dry creek bed next to it. I did not want to do this. I felt pressed to complete my other planting before dark, and moving the yucca over would then crowd the grasses. Failing to dissuade him, however, I then tried to move this somewhat large and unwieldly plant. Inadvertantly and to my great dismay, I snapped off the end of the vulnerable taproot. I should have resisted his pressure and moved the plant the next day when I had more time, energy, and patience. As it was, I resented giving in to his seemingly insensitive demand and regretted my own carelessness. Over-reacting in my exhaustion, I stomped off in anger and disgust, calling back over my shoulder that we should just throw the yucca away because it would probably die anyway.

As soon as Forrest retreated from the garden, I found the nearest bench and sat down to collect myself. It wasn't easy. I already knew I would have to work until dark to finish my other work. But, in sitting for a few minutes, at least I could discharge the bulk of my anger, analyze the nature

of my emotional response, and articulate in words how I would choose to discuss this incident with Forrest at the appropriate time. As I sat there, I couldn't help but notice all the beautiful flowers blooming so profusely, and the sky and trees aglow with the warm, golden light of the setting sun. In witnessing the calm face of Nature and listening to Her soothing voice, my damaged feelings began to repair themselves. I could feel myself "falling in love anew," as Forrest puts it, with this divine relationship with Creation. The next day I learned that Forrest, too, had found his own place of refuge that evening on a bench in another part of the garden, no doubt salving his own wounds at my hands. And he carefully replanted the damaged yucca, which appears to be doing fine. Another lesson learned.

In reflection of this experience, I can't help but wonder, considering the high price of therapy these days, if people couldn't better empower themselves and save money by letting their garden be their "therapist" in certain matters. One could save the cost of just one or two sessions, for example, and buy a good bench that would provide years of soulful comforting.

I am quite clear that Forrest and I could not and would not have created such a powerful sanctuary if, in our heart of hearts, we did not need it so very much. If we have more sitting areas than any garden I've ever seen of similar size, it's because we know how very much we need the haven they provide for us. Our sitting areas allow us to contemplate and admire the many visages that Nature presents to us, each symbolizing yet another quality that we revere and aspire to possess (we even have a tiny bench hidden from view just for visiting dwarfs or fairies).

Once you accept that your Sanctuary Garden, however nobly intended to honor Nature, can also serve as an arena for soothing wounds within yourself or with others, your relationship with your garden will become even deeper. No doubt there will be ample opportunity to use it in such a context, as you surrender to Nature's amazing capacity to absorb your personal imperfections as well as those of the world. That is as worthy a use for sanctuary as when you go to your garden to pray or meditate.

Indeed, just having a Sanctuary Garden and a calming place to sit within its boundaries, will make you, in time, a more forgiving person. One day you may also discover that you feel more loving, more tolerant, or perhaps more flexible and more at peace with yourself and others. You will recognize within you an amazing devotion to preserving this sense of growing peace that perhaps before seemed rather unattainable. Entwined within this devotion to peace will be an unshakable devotion to place—your own Sanctuary Garden and the Earth that cradles it, for which you are the loving steward. Perhaps one day soon you will count your blessings that you had the wisdom to give yourself the sanctuary that surely we are each meant to have in this life.

7

Natural Features:
Wood and Stone

Trees are sanctuaries. Whoever knows how to speak to them,
whoever knows how to listen to them, can learn the truth.
They do not preach learning and precepts, they preach
undeterred by particulars, the ancient law of life.

—HERMANN HESSE,

Wandering

I had to make a confession of faith in stone.

—CARL JUNG

I must confess, I know little about plants from the perspective of a gardener. Instead their names come to me spontaneously on a stroll of childlike wonderment—"little bright eyes," "yellow puff," "dancing one," and the like. My ignorance of proper names betrays me when visitors arrive and ask "What's this and what's that?" I don't know, I say, you must ask Tricia about such matters.

But point to a piece of wood, a rock, or even the effects of the wind, ah. Then my heart leaps and my eyes widen with excitement. These natural features are my particular varieties of "plants." Tricia willingly stains her knees and dirties her hands performing the marriage of plant to soil. She sits and meditates with flowers, receiving their subtle psychical vibration. Her oneness with plants has allowed her to rekindle an ancient wisdom about the healing properties of flower essences.

As for me, my baptism in the garden comes regularly by yoking my body and soul to the form of rock and wood in their fully natural states. These are my teachers. If I am wiser as a gardener, it is because I have surrendered to the ancient knowledge hidden in the so-called bones of the garden—those elements of rock and wood as they find form in fences, trellises, borders, water features, paths, among many other possibilities.

On the evolutionary scale, flowers are relatively new to the Earth, appearing not too long before humans, but trees are great ancestors and rock even greater. For me, therefore, the garden becomes more natural, magical, *and* sacred when adorned with wood and stone. Religious historian Mircea Eliade, in his book, *Myths, Dreams, and Mysteries,* underscores this thought: "The sacred tree, the sacred stone are not adored as stone or tree; they are worshipped precisely because they are hierophanies, because they show something that is no longer stone or tree but *sacred,* the *ganz andere* or 'wholly other.'" Of course, metal, when sculpted and sensitively displayed in art pieces, is magnetic as well. And wind, when captured in chimes, trees, leaves, whispy grasses, and

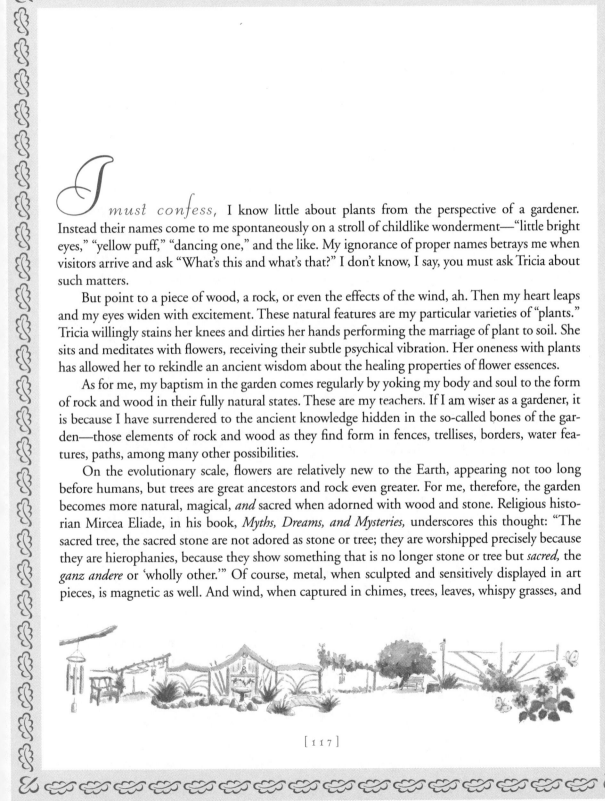

even whimsical garden ornaments has its own kinetic splendor. The Sanctuary Garden, however, is the place and opportunity for its Keeper to become like a jeweler, designing and placing those natural wooden and mineral gems of Nature in a setting that draws admiration and adoration.

TOUCHSTONES OF SPIRIT

As a young boy, I was stopped on my way to China by a rock—at the bottom of a two-foot-deep hole in my backyard. I was astonished to discover it as if it were some buried treasure now exposed to the sun for the first time in probably thousands of years. I filled in the hole and went about my daily activities.

One activity—marbles—especially delighted me. For years I not only collected gemlike marbles but also marble-sized stones. I carried the stones in a pouch separate from my marbles. They were used to mark the perimeter of the game circle. Over the years, I developed a keen eye for finding a particularly nice stone. My friends came to value not only my taste in marbles but also my stones. Upon finding one I would place it in my right front pocket. I soon made a mental note to keep that pocket special—only for stones.

My walks home from school were like scavenger hunts for these unique pebbles. Little did I know that years later I would outgrow these streets and replace them with trails, following my true passion for hiking and a much more intimate experience with rocks and mountains.

To this day, I still have a sacred front pocket for a few touchstones. I have found some marvelous ones and very plain ones. I have given many away and lost some. But it is their comfort I gain throughout the day that is so special—feeling, smoothing, tracking an indentation here and a crack there, imagining the stone's shading in my mind as I caress its body.

Everytime I touch one of my touchstones I say a prayer—a carryover of childhood when I would make a silent wish for luck in a game, or to gain God's protection from my father's wrath.

Over the years, I have learned that a stone has a great holding capacity for faith and perserverence. And in its muteness it has a great memory for things long past.

Everyone needs a special stone. Place a stone in your pocket as a symbol of sanctuary. You are a garden yourself worthy of sacredness. Nurture your mind, heart, and soul in this small way and you will become a jeweler of your own divine spirit.

If we are to deny the power, beauty, and function of well-placed rocks and stones in a Sanctuary Garden, we may indeed be refuting our own sacred kinship with them and their ancestoral holiness. Mythological historian Joseph Campbell concurs: "The manifestation of the sacred in a stone or a tree is neither less mysterious nor less noble than its manifestation as a 'god.'"

Rock Rules

How do you go about selecting a rock for your sanctuary with reverent intent? Here are some simple rules guaranteed to make it a "moving" experience.

Rule 1: Remember that rocks are beings, too. They just don't move much, take a *long* time to age, have few expectations, and are generally quite content wherever they happen to be.

Rule 2: Choose a rock when everything is quiet—inside *you*. Especially important: don't let anybody help you choose.

Rule 3: Get down close to the Earth and smell the place of the rock—where it lives and breathes and goes about its business. Notice the many little friends (bugs, etc.) who have made their home in the shelter of this rock.

Rule 4: You have to look a rock right in the eye—up close and personal. Talk to it, explain your purpose in using it, ask permission, and then ask for its blessing. Is this too much to ask?

Rule 5: If somebody asks you, "What's so special about that rock?" don't tell them. Nobody is supposed to know what's special about another person's rock. This is a secret between you and your rock.

Consciously place a rock in your garden and you have created a small shrine—an anchor to God, the stars, this Earth, and yourself.

Stretch your imagination for a moment, and discover that your body is actually made of rock fragmented over eons into soil, organized into plants, and finding newfound freedom and mobility as a human animal (the thirteenth-century Persian mystic poet, Rumi, reminds us "We began as a mineral. We emerged into plant life and into animal state, and then into being human . . ."). You carry within your body those same minerals of your rock ancestors, as do all plants. And you are most certainly made of the stuff of stars. In an inspiring unpublished essay titled "The Shrine of the Mountain and the Waters," Oregon architect Tom Bender reminds us that the rocks that constitute the mantle of our planet are the ashes of long dead stars. "The stars of today are in fact our cousins, and rocks under our feet are our geological grandparents and our genealogical link with the canopy of stars over our heads."

Traditional peoples resorted to great stone structures to contact the spirit world, to dream, to

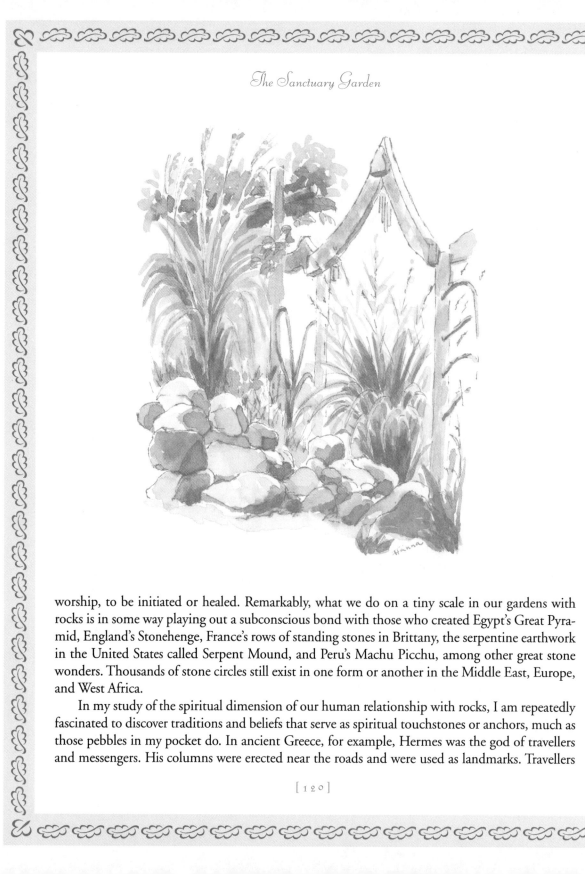

worship, to be initiated or healed. Remarkably, what we do on a tiny scale in our gardens with rocks is in some way playing out a subconscious bond with those who created Egypt's Great Pyramid, England's Stonehenge, France's rows of standing stones in Brittany, the serpentine earthwork in the United States called Serpent Mound, and Peru's Machu Picchu, among other great stone wonders. Thousands of stone circles still exist in one form or another in the Middle East, Europe, and West Africa.

In my study of the spiritual dimension of our human relationship with rocks, I am repeatedly fascinated to discover traditions and beliefs that serve as spiritual touchstones or anchors, much as those pebbles in my pocket do. In ancient Greece, for example, Hermes was the god of travellers and messengers. His columns were erected near the roads and were used as landmarks. Travellers passing by threw rocks at the feet of these columns. This custom is also followed in Tibet, where each traveller crossing the high mountain passes leaves a rock on the cairn at the top.

Inspired by these traditions, Tricia and I began erecting a cairn at Cortesia, inside that part of the garden called The Shrine. Still in its infancy, visitors are welcome to place stones atop it, and they even have the opportunity to inscribe a prayer or thought on the stone before it is placed.

For me, this gesture of honoring stone comes natural. John Lame Deer, a Sioux Medicine Man, reminds us that *inyan*—the rocks—are holy. Therefore, every person needs a stone to help him. In his book, *Lame Deer, Seeker of Visions,* Lame Deer explains: "You are always picking up odd-shaped stones, pebbles and fossils, saying that you do this because it pleases you, but I know better. Deep inside you there must be an awareness of the rock power, of the spirits in them, otherwise you would not pick them up and fondle them as you do." Even the Native American, Chief Seattle, in his famous speech of 1854 remarked that "the rocks, which seem to be dumb as they swelter in the sun along the silent shore, thrill with memories of stirring events connected with the lives of my people." Indeed, to the Native Americans, the "rock people" are sacred beings. For the Oglala Sioux, one of the four powers which together are called *Wakan tanka* (the Great Spirit) is "the Rock," which *was* even before Earth's creation and is the oldest of material things.

Perhaps the purest example of the religious importance of a rock is The Rock of Ishi in Japan. At the Ishi Shrine, there is no inner-shrine building at all, only a fence enclosing a large rock. People come to this rock with humility and bow before it with respect. Its antiquity cannot even be historically traced. The Rock of Ishi represents creative divinity as the soil. Here Shinto belief declares man is not an outlaw in the universe but is one with universal divinity.

This begs the question: What gives a stone a perceived sense of importance and power? Obviously, I have lived with a lifelong curiosity about this. The answer seems rather simple: our own human intent to see in this artifact of Nature something eternal—our Self. But for the moment, this seems too human-centered an explanation. I like the hypothetical explanation from the point of view of a rock that physicist Itzhak Bentov offered years ago in his classic *Stalking the Wild Pendulum.*

Sticking his neck out as a "metaphysical physicist," Bentov postulated that matter contains consciousness, and if there is enough critical mass of this consciousness then a dim awareness of self will develop. Over millions of years this dim awareness may be strengthened into a sharper identity possibly through interaction with other creatures. Here's Bentov's vision:

Imagine a rock in a cleft of which an animal finds refuge. The animal feels grateful to the rock, and the rock dimly registers that appreciation. Later, a bird makes its nest there and gives birth to new life. This boosts the rock's ego considerably, increasing its consciousness quotient. Sooner or later, Bentov suggests, the consciousness of the rock will evolve into a *spirit of the rock.* More and more creatures are attracted to the rock and its consciousness continues to increase. When at last a human being encounters the rock, that person will sense something special about the place. More and more people will come to the rock. Before long there is a "cult" going and this boosts the ego of the *spirit of the rock* immensely because the thoughts of the people who concentrate on her adds to her power . . . she is stimulated by the level of energy produced by the human nervous system. Eventually, *the spirit of the rock,* which started out as a vague, dim awareness in a mass of matter, develops into a powerful spirit or a tribal god (or even a small marketing hit, as with the "Pet Rock" of the 1970's).

Indeed, we are all spiritual beings on a journey to find the temple of the Divine. Rocks, trees, animals, humans—along the way we eventually find some comfort in sanctuary. And in that sacred place we find meaning in our own way. As a philosopher, gardener, and spiritual aspirant, I must not forget that I am a member of a vast tribe of only twenty to forty human generations that have roamed this Earth. Somehow, if I forget my relationship to stone, I forget my past. And in forgetting my past I lose any connection to a "stone of power"—my own sense of eternal divine royalty.

The magic in a stone is its simple unpretentious sort of existence: In any condition—as pebble, massive boulder, sculpture, even tombstone—it is complete, suggesting a type of permanence. We could live a thousand lifetimes, return to the same rock, and find, perhaps, that it has not changed at all. Its wholeness appears unchanging and lasting. It is for this reason that human history is steeped in recognizing and honoring the symbolic essence of stones.

The medieval alchemical philosopher's stone (lapis) was the pre-eminent symbol of our human wholeness, and that which can never be lost or dissolved—our immortal and unalterable mystical relationship to God. And the process of rubbing such a stone (or any smooth, round stone, for that matter) was akin to polishing one's Self, that is, the eternal reflective Spirit of God, which mirrors our wholeness. The ancients afforded similar spiritual connotations to crystal. A crystal represents one's Self as the nuclear center of our physical existence: the union of extreme opposites, of matter and spirit. The mathematically precise arrangement of a crystal evokes in us the intuitive feeling that even in so-called "dead" matter (as suggested, perhaps falsely, in a rock), there is a spiritual ordering principle at work.

Years ago, a dear friend, Barbara, gifted our garden with a sizable piece of quartz. Immediately I saw in it the opportunity to honor the power and presence of this cosmic duality of matter and spirit. Placed on a stump just inside the formal garden, its pure, white beauty is the first image perceived by the visitor. Only recently has another stone of conspicuous power found its resting place in our garden. It is a large piece of sculpted granite called the *Narana Stone.* Out of a rounded smoothness, almost like a silken shawl, appears an upturned face—Narana's profile—looking slightly heavenward. I have chosen not to tell anyone, not even Tricia, about my discovery of this mystical stone. The Narana Stone sits in the herb garden commanding her own eastward attention. Nearby is our wisteria arbor and a lone contemplative bench. The magnetism of this stone is felt in fully one-half of the garden. And its unique sculpture lends an element of mysticism: From the Shrine Garden you look down on her backside and see only a standing smooth oblong rock, no facial profile; from other angles you catch unique images.

Mystery aside, I cannot pass up an opportunity to share the spiritual significance of such a rock, and to encourage you to find your own unique stone of power for your Sanctuary Garden. The Narana Stone is a reminder that inside each of us is our perfect Self, an already perfect sculpture of our unrealized potential. Too often our preoccupation with worldly matters prevents us from touching and sensing the hidden image of the Divine within, but the vision of a sculptor can, serving to release the prize of a stone from its imprisonment.

I am inclined to believe that there is a Great Sculptor at work in the universe, shaping, touching, polishing all of life in Her image. Each of us is a work in progress, a pouring out of God's love. Dante intuitively echoed the process at work in our becoming, although he was referring to paint-

Rock and Wood for the Soul

The spiritual symbolism held within stone and wood (especially trees) has a long history in most cultures. Here are a few ways a stone, tree, or piece of wood may touch your spirit.

ROCKS

- Depicts our eternal or Divine nature.
- Depicts completeness or permanence.
- Depicts our immortal, unalterable mystical relationship to God.
- As a crystal, symbolizes the unification of matter and spirit.
- Depicts our perfect Self and our unrealized potential.
- Is a touchstone of spirit or prophecy.

WOOD

- Image of the cosmos or universe.
- Is a dwelling place of informed spirits.
- A medium of prophecy, knowledge, wisdom.
- Symbol of metamorphosis, rebirth.
- Symbol of growth, proliferation.
- As a Sacred Tree, symbolizes a safe haven, home, hearth, or sanctuary in which to find healing, power, wisdom, and security.

ing. He said, "He who would paint a figure, if he cannot become that figure, cannot portray it." So it is that God, as the Great Sculptor, cannot portray us if He cannot become us. Think about this as you create your Sanctuary Garden. Here is an opportunity to honor the gemstone that is your own Divinity through those rocks and special stones you bring into your garden.

One Christmas, I gave Tricia a coupon saying I would move one rock a day into the garden for the next three months. The task actually had a practical side to it: the garden, in fact, did need more rocks for borders, and the bordering forest had a few too many rocks to make strolling through it leisurely. Soon, however, I became more bound up in the ritual of the duty than I had originally expected.

At first, I thought rock moving to be a rather benign form of exercise. But then something got hold of me. I realized that it was the ritual of anticipation, of dressing up gruffly for just one rock, of meandering into the woods, and thoughtfully observing which rock would be selected and relocated. This ritual was about feeling the density of matter in a deliberate way that tested my own strength and stamina. And it was about talking to a particualr rock, explaining my purpose, receiving its permission, and carrying it in my arm, like holding a tired child on a hike. Indeed, this ritual came to symbolize for me the transporting of a sacred object to and from the altar, where distance is second to determination, and determination is second to devotion.

Needless to say, many months passed, outdating my original coupon obligation. And still the ritual of mindful rock moving continued. In all fairness to Tricia's own fortitude, I want to point out that moving rocks was not my venue alone. Tricia has done her great share, wheelbarrowing them down through the forest, heaving them over fencelines, and prying them up out of the ground in a new bed, as if delivering a newborn child. But for me, my soul was caught up in something here. I can only try to do justice to it by speaking about it once again in spiritual terms.

I believe Earth/Nature is our sacred talisman, a touchstone of our universal subconscious need to touch, embrace, hold, feel, and relate to the Source of our existence. We pass through Nature's hands in our journey for understanding in this life but, more than that, Earth/Nature passes through our own human hands, like a talisman, seeking to pass its magical knowing to we who wish to receive it. In truth, all knowledge is merely borrowed so that we may find truth in it and pass that truth on to others.

For those of us who seek or have been touched by that underlying spirit of all existence, we discover that Earth is a generous giver. She does not hold on desperately to what is rightfully hers. She yields to our human needs, appearing if not unattached then seemingly indifferent to our actions.

But the Cortesian way of life is based not on ruthless and endless taking. It is founded on gestures of respect and honor upholding a relationship of reverence. If there is an exchange between beings, it is based on "borrowing only that which you can use." In a reciprocal, courteous

WITH FIR BRANCHES (OR ANY), FLAT ROCKS, & 1×2's,
YOU CAN MAKE A SIMPLE STAIRWAY WITH RAILING
LEADING TO A FOCAL POINT

exchange we appeal to another being and seek permission to borrow their energy. The duty of borrowing, therefore, implies integrity of use—upholding a being's honor.

This agreement between human and stone is exemplified here at Cortesia. In my wildest dreams I would not have expected to have had such a mindful relationship to rocks in a garden. We have gone beyond mere rock borders and the occassional anchor rock in a bed. The size, texture, shape, and color all reflect the drama of a rock's location—the color of plants, soil, lighting during different times of the day, and so on. In the woodland garden many of the rocks are old, decaying basalt, their skin scarred and cracked and adorned with moss, lichen, and parasitical vegetation. There are powerful icon rocks positioned as if they had been there for centuries, yet placed purposely to force your attention. Even the springlike ponds and watercourses are as much epiphanies to rocks as they are to water. Indeed, we garden as much to nurture rocks in our sanctuary as we do plants, water, wood, and wildlife.

A few years ago, however, we created a rock feature that speaks to the core of our celebration of rock—a dry creek bed, approximately sixty feet in length, which bisects part of the garden flowing from an upper area known as The Shrine. Of all our rock creations, this dry creek bed holds the most meaning to me. On one hand, it represents the illusion that is life—the Eastern mystical premise that we are just dreams in the mind of God. No water flows through this creek, yet it unmistakably suggests water's (God's) fertile presence. The more hidden meaning of the creek, on the other hand, has to do with my personal quest for mindfulness in all that I do.

I was inspired to create this dry creek based on an experience I had many years ago while doing a solo hike into the mountains of Los Angeles. I had hiked for miles up a canyon stepping on nothing but the many-sized rocks of a dry creek bed. It was not a leisurely stroll to be sure, but rather forced my attention at each step, lest I slip and sprain an ankle. At first my attention was sloppy and errant, but then I found my focus, as draining as it was over time. My perserverance paid off for, to my astonishment, at a certain point a gushing stream appeared from beneath the surface of rocks, flowed for awhile, disappeared, then reappeared again up the canyon. To my great content, this pattern continued for a few miles, finally ending at a deep pool.

The secret of my passion with rock and wood in the garden is a heightened state of mindfulness and reverence through Nature. The mind–state of which I speak is perhaps best characterized by the Zen concept of "bare attention." This is a quality of awareness that keeps us sparkling alive and attentive to the present moment, feeling the pregnant fullness of what is happening. We observe things as they are. We do not choose, compare, evaluate, project, or lay down expectations with a reactive mind. No. A leaf falls from a tree, lands on the water, and floats away. We are one with our foot as it lands on a rock pad, but we leave that present moment behind as we float now with our other foot, performing its allotted duty.

Bare attention is what brings our forever thinking, reactive mind to rest, even as it appears that we are still using it to plant a foot here and another foot there. It is this special blending of our mind and body with the environment in such a spontaneous here-and-now manner which moves us along in an intuitive-experiential state of mindfulness. This is surely the very state of mind we dove into as a child aimlessly kicking a rock down the street. Seemingly without effort, we just went along, but spontaneously so, our whole world of feelings and thoughts contracted into a full silent awareness of only *that* rock, only *that* street, and only *our* foot. In such a bare attention, we become one with the moment—a moment that is simple, magically balanced in intent, peacefully restful, yet intuitively directed as effortless effort.

Can you grasp the full power of such effort in Nature? An effort which becomes effortless in its spontaneity and freedom? Instead, we are more inclined to cling to life with a judging and reactive mind. We dwell in the past, mulling over what has already happened, and we get lost in the worry, anxiety, fear or fantasy of what is to come.

By taking sanctuary in Nature, we enter Her with a different need: to be here now in the present moment of peace, comfort, awe and wonder, appreciation and gratitude. This is a mind at rest from the world, a mind fully on another scale of attentiveness. Indeed, Tricia and I have created each Sanctuary Garden design element as a means to make it easier to come back into mindful balance with Nature, God, and our souls. In the Sanctuary Garden it is much easier to surrender to Nature as our teacher and guide. We replace apprehension with curiosity, and fear with trust. By forming a partnership with stone, plants, wood, water, and the like, we learn to live simply and think even more simple.

All of this allows us, as our garden's Keeper, to dive into the geometry and color of a flower *without thinking about* geometry or color. With bare attention and a mindful heart, we can dive into the glistening pearl of morning dew, the warmth of a sunbeam piercing the forest veil, the scent of wild roses mingling with pine and lavender. We can observe a rock, pick it up, carry it, and put in down as if it were the only rock on Earth we were asked to befriend. All of this, and infinitely more in Nature, is the romance of our mind and heart and spirit. And to casually pass it all by is to miss a throbbing beat from the bosom of the Divine Mother.

SANCTUARY OF WOOD

Among the touchstones in my right-front pocket is one item of special significance to me—a pebble-sized wooden burl. The day I found it—many years ago—my gaze and hand seemed to be thrust to the forest floor and, among all the duff, guided to this wooden gem. Upon it is naturally inscribed undecipherable runes that only its Mother Tree could decode—swirllike fingerprints as of a universe begging to find form, swirls as if they were prayers from a distant god or instructions on how to get along in life.

I am afraid I am very attached to this burl pebble. It speaks for all the passion that is my name—Forrest—and for perhaps my deepest bond with Nature and this Earth: trees.

I implore you to find a deep covenant with wood in your Sanctuary Garden, and to understand and pray for the security of all trees in this Earth Sanctuary. This planet's forests, and especially those rainforests of the tropics and temperate forests of the Northern Hemisphere, are the lungs of this Earth, oxygenating the air we breathe, regulating our climate, providing food and shelter for most of this world's vital animal life, and creating the greatest diversity of plant life ever imagined. Just as with water and air, the quality of life on Earth can be measured by the health of Her forests.

My own relationship to wood in our Sanctuary Garden is an outgrowth of my deep honoring of tree beings. My spiritual bond with them is worthy of many more words than I have the space here to share. You will most certainly find your unique application and interpretation of wood as a feature in your own garden. But let me encourage you to find that place inside your soul that sees wood not purely for its utilitarian value. Our human relationship with trees also has a long legacy of deep, spiritual significance. Indeed, our every action can be said to be an outcome of our relationship in some way to that mystical Tree of Life in Eden.

The groundwork for my passion for wood was laid as an adolescent. I gained respect for trees in one dramatic moment when I was about six years old. More out of defiance and show-offing than courage, I climbed to the uppermost branches of a stately oak tree. I reveled in the sinewy feel of limb and rough bark, even imagining the air to be cleaner and crisper in this upper story of Heaven—and then I fell. I did not hit the ground, but was rather pummelled by the outstretched limbs until finally I came to rest in a secure crotch.

The fact is, I was alone in this ordeal, with no onlookers to rescue me. And that, I submit, was my blessing. My bruised ego (and body) had to find solace in the comfort of this tree. And that was when trees began to speak to my soul.

A few years later, as I shared in the introduction to this book, I began almost a fifteen-year mecca to a wooded shrine in the backyard of our new suburban home. My relationship with this birch, as an asylum from incessant conflict in our family, infused me with a powerful compassion for life. Enfolded by her shade, the Birch Goddess taught me about respect and love, but mostly about forgiving. Her silent comfort stilled my angry and confused mind. She spoke through the wind in the spring, the birds in summer, Her leaves at my feet in fall, and Her stark white naked countenance in winter. More than anything, however, She spoke to me through my guitar. I can only say that holding a finely crafted wooden instrument at your breast every day for over thirty-eight years, as I have, and feeling its vibration enter your heart through song, is truly a divine way to celebrate our human and soulful connection to Nature and God.

The Birch Goddess watched me grow from a boy into a young man, even as she herself began as but a princess five- or six-feet tall upon her arrival, and as an elegant queen of thirty to forty feet saw me off to marriage.

Just as we need a small, simple stone in our pocket, each of us needs the sanctuary of a tree. Herein lies another anchor for our soul. As the Keeper of our soul-garden and our garden's sanctuary, we need a Tree of Life to find spiritual sustenance and to remind us we are not alone. We need to know that God lives in Nature around us, alive with skin, texture, light, color, and musk. A tree or a piece of wood is a splendid image of God we should want to honor in the garden that is our life.

Among archetypal images, the Sacred Tree is one of the most widely known symbols on Earth. There are few cultures in which the Sacred Tree does not figure: as an image of the cosmos, as a dwelling place of gods or spirits, as a medium of prophecy and knowledge, and as an agent of metamorphoses when the tree is transformed into human or divine form or when it bears a divine or human image as its fruit or flower.

The "cult of trees," for example, has always been important in Indian religion. In the Bhagavadgita, the tree represents the universe—the giant fig tree, Aswattha: "The everlasting, rooted in heaven, its branches earthward: each of its leaves is a song of the Vedas, and he who knows it knows all the Vedas." The Yakshi or tree goddess is the indwelling spirit of the sacred tree. The

Buddha was born as his mother was clasping a *sal* tree. He received enlightenment under the Bodhi Tree, and he died on a couch set among a grove of *sal* trees.

Be it the *neotemes,* or sacred groves of Celtic lore, the Lote Tree in the Koran, which signifies the bounds of spiritual knowledge beyond which man may not pass, or even the Tree of the Knowledge of Good and Evil common to the Judeo, Christian, and Islamic myth of Eden— humans seem to need to sacralize a tree as a symbol of rebirth, growth, proliferation, and inexhaustible life; indeed, of prophecy and divination.

There are many myths and stories of trees that speak and sing. Each implies that housed within is an intelligence or spirit. The oracle at the oaks of Dodona sacred to Zeus spoke through the creaking of the boughs, the rustling of leaves, and the humming of bronze gongs suspended from limbs. King David himself would listen to the rustling of mulberry leaves in order to hear the voice of God. In Western literature, we are reminded of the Wood of the Suicides in Dante's *Inferno,* Spenser's *Faery Queen,* and even the Ents or tree shepherds in Tolkien's *Lord of the Rings.*

In his compelling book about the archetype of the green man throughout modern history, *Green Man*, William Anderson captures the mysticism of Nature speaking to us through trees:

"When we stand beneath a copse of beeches roaring in a high wind, we seem to hear one of the voices of Nature only our innermost being can comprehend. It sends a message that indicates that nothing we claim for ourselves is ours . . . and that we are rooted only for a short time in history, far shorter than the lives of the beeches singing and chanting above us. When we surrender our hearts and minds to their sounds, we undergo a purification which is tinged with the feeling of sacrifice and making holy everything we have been given."

When I walk into a forest, when I see a tree or hold in my hands a piece of wood, I feel enfolded, brought in and gathered from the world. I can touch the wisdom inside my soul that speaks like rings of cycles of reincarnations. It is the silent knowledge of seasons past, of many different moons.

For me the lone, stalwart tree is one of the strongest images of sanctuary to find comfort in. Recently, on a late-summer trip to the family cabin high up in the Rockies, I stood on a solitary peak at 10,000 feet—alone with the skeletal remains of a solitary juniper. Reciting by heart Omar Khayyam's epic mystical poem *The Rubaiyat,* I received great inspiration and insight from this tree that has been ravished for years by the harshest wind, rain, snow, sun, and lightning. It was as if all my incarnations sat before me listening, huddled at that juniper's lap, clinging to its tendril-like roots, which themselves clasp only to the life force of rocky granite. This juniper saw every sunrise and sunset I missed my whole life, and then some.

In many ways this juniper reflected the insight of my literary mentor, Hermann Hesse, who observed in his meditative book *Wandering,* "A tree says: My strength is trust. I know nothing about my fathers, I know nothing about the thousand children that every year spring out of me. I live out the secret of my seed to the very end, and I care for nothing else. I trust that God is in me. I trust that my labor is holy. Out of this trust I live."

It is absolutely impossible to not be profoundly struck by the cathedral-like woods at Cortesia. These sentinals of fir, maple, and oak ring and guard our gardens. Our gardens, in fact, grow ceremoniously at the floor of these pillars. By living day and night among such a setting, I have gained a sense of humility not unlike a priest daily awakening to serve God's mighty hall. Living here has tempered that great sense of woundedness and anger many of us environmentalists feel over the destruction of old-growth forests throughout the world. It is hard to explain, but in honoring the woods I steward daily, I have humbly embraced both their useful and "useless" nature. In doing so, I am guided by a tale told by the famous Chinese sage, Chuang-Tzu:

A carpenter called Stone was traveling with his apprentice and saw standing in a field, near an earth altar, a large old oak tree. It stood crooked and bent with every branch gnarled and twisted. The carpenter said to his apprentice, who was, surprisingly, admiring the tree: "This is a stupid useless oak tree. Why, if you wanted to make a ship, it would soon rot and sink; if you wanted to make tools, they would break beyond repair. You can't find any use with this tree, and that's why it has become ugly and old."

But, that night, the carpenter went to sleep and the old oak tree appeared to him in his dream and said: "You stupid man, why do you compare me to your cultivated trees, your cinnamon, pear, orange, apple trees, and all others which bear fruit and are useful? Even before they can ripen their fruit, people attack and plunder them, breaking their branches, and tearing at their twigs and leaves. Their own gifts bring harm to them and they cannot live out their natural life span. That is what happens everywhere, and that is why I have long since tried to become useless. You stupid creature, imagine if I had been useful, would I have been able to grow this big and this old? But, even so, you and I are both creatures, and how can one creature set himself so high as to judge another? You useless mortal man, what do you know about useless trees?"

Needless to say, the next morning, the carpenter awoke and meditated on his dream, and found a deep change of heart toward the old oak tree. When his apprentice again asked him just

Aesthetic and Practical Values of Rock and Wood in Your Yard or Garden

- · Enhances the drama of a setting.
- · Gives visual relief from plants and flowers.
- · Accents vegetation or other features.
- · Provides artful variety.
- · Is more natural and rustic looking.
- · Provides useful perches for birds, butterflies, insects.
- · Is useful for borders and paths.
- · Shades and protects exposed soil.
- · Provides a strong anchor point to attract the eye.
- · Very economical and longlasting.
- · Provides a creative outlet for personal expression.

why this one tree served to protect the earth altar, if in fact it were so useless, Stone answered, "Shut up! Say no more! Every man knows how useful it is to be useful. No one seems to know how useful it is to be useless!"

Most people measure the value of wood by its usefulness or uselessness. In the many natural features at Cortesia in which I honor wood—fences, screens, trellises, benches, borders, arbors, sitting platforms, decaying logs in beds, and natural debris integrated with ponds and watercourses—I have made every conscious attempt to use the wood our land gives us without predetermined judgement. When the natural forest debris—shattered and fallen limbs, decaying stumps, and the like—is elevated to a whole other level in my features, you would never once consider their original "useless" nature. Yet, unfortunately, most people would pass such wood by or consider hauling it away or chipping it up into bark mulch.

I challenge you to honor wood in your outdoor sanctuary in creative, heartfelt ways. It is not always necessary to invest in your local lumberyard. The features you create out of natural wood, in the many forms you find it, will give your setting a magnetic personality.

The natural woven fence I created along a thirty-foot stretch of the entrance is entirely made from loosely woven wild-hazelnut switches. I select the green switches, about one-half to three-quarters of an inch thick, from the wild bushes that grow on our land. But I only take one or two from each plant upon asking permission and explaining their use. The woven effect is startling to the eye, as if gazing through transparent stained-glass panels. The woven tinsel has also proven to keep deer out. I received my inspiration for such a use of wood by noticing how vegetation in a natural setting does not grow strictly vertically or horizontally, as one would likely construct a wooden or wire fence. Read Nature's drama—her forms curve, spiral, lean, and contort in a dance or rhythm of design and function. From a distance you cannot make out my fence from the foliage behind it. It all moves together and gives the illusion of a live fence, which is my next project in the garden—replacing the south facing fenceline with live weavings of willow and other shrubs.

Broken or shattered fallen limbs provide another opportunity for creativity in the garden. One winter an ice storm shattered limbs from some oaks in the front meadow. Demoralized by the destruction, it took me over a year to finally clean up the debris. But I needed that time, I guess, to heal a bit from the event. Just at the time I had created the new outer-garden entrance threshold nearer the house, I had removed those old geometrically clever batwing gates from the entrance to the formal garden in the meadow. Suddenly, I remembered the shattered oak limbs and in my mind saw their perfect use: as a natural archway into the formal garden. With hanging Tibetan bells, this particular entrance has a strong magnetic organic energy. So, I placed a little one-seat stump-bench there for any visiting elves or Nature Spirits to sit. Recently, some twisted branches from another tree shattered and very quickly became just the trellis I had been looking for to train one of Tricia's clematises up the side of the garden shed.

Fallen and shattered wood integrates well with the earth. It can be partially buried, giving the illusion of emerging out of the soil. Such wood, as lengths of tree trunks, are incredible resources for garden beds. They decompose slowly and, in the process, create niches in which parasitic vegetation can grow. They are also apt to

NATURAL FIR/MADRONE ARCH (BARK LEFT ON) WITH FEVERFEW + 'STIPA GIGANTEA' GRASS

develop a mossy texture in wet climates. They are worthy icons in a flower bed, and serve to relieve the eye from all the vegetation. They are also great little perches for butterflies and birds.

Dotted around our gardens are several stumps, some to sit on, others with water bowls, and still others serving as simple earth altars on which we occassionally place an assortment of Nature objects—leaves, stones, flowers, dead bugs, crystals, twigs, and others. If you ever need to deal with a tree that you absolutely *must* remove, save its trunk for cut-up stumps. These make great flower stands, seats and the like. Also consider leaving eight feet or so of the trunk of a removed tree still standing. This type of snag will be greatly appreciated by wildlife, and if you place a birdhouse atop it, as we did to one such tree, you will have immediate visitors.

Perhaps my greatest delight in creating natural wooden features has been in the use of fir limbs that have fallen to the ground in our woods. Years ago, I began collecting them, inspired by their slightly curved nature. These have been the inspiration for several trellises in which the limbs form a natural curved fan. Visitors see this fan effect as sort of a theme in my wooden art.

When honoring wood in your garden, celebrate all aspects of it. Wood has incredible texture, both visual and tactile. My rough-sawn bench near the entrace begs for its hide to be stroked. Our smooth-skinned driftwood pieces are not only whimsical but invite the casual touch. The colors of bark are enhanced by lighting and moisture, so consider varieties of vegetation, as we have, that show off their skin. A fine wooden bench also showcases the grain and form of its parent tree. Whether weathered or preserved to enhance the wood, a well-placed wooden bench is a natural draw for the weary pilgrim.

The American Indians had a place in their mythology for the Sacred Tree. The tree was like a home, a sanctuary for creation on Earth. It especially held the power of a hearth around which, under which, all the people of the Earth may gather to find healing, power, wisdom, and security. The Creator planted the Sacred Tree. Its roots spread deep into the body of Mother Earth. Its branches reach upward like hands praying to Father Sky. The fruits of this tree are the good things the Creator has given to the people: teachings that show the path to love, compassion, generosity, patience, wisdom, justice, courage, respect, humility, and many other wonderful gifts.

The ancient ones taught that the life of the Tree is the life of the people. If the people wander far away from the protective shadow of the Tree, they wander into worldly delusion. In John Neihardt's eloquent biography, *Black Elk Speaks*, the great Native-American chief Black Elk spoke of a vision he had which capsulates the power of the Sacred Tree:

Then I was standing on the highest mountain of them all, and round about beneath me was the whole hoop of the world. And while I stood there I saw more than I can tell and I understood more than I saw: for I was seeing in a sacred manner the shapes of all things in the spirit, and the shape of all shapes as they must live together like one being. And I saw that the sacred hoop of my people was one of many hoops that made one circle, wide as daylight and as starlight, and in the center grew one mighty flowering tree to shelter all the children of one mother and one father. And I saw that it was holy.

Out of our need for sanctuary, we need to feel at one again with home. How many of us ever consider that our abode—itself constructed of myriad pieces of wood—is but an opportunity to live inside the Sacred Tree? In this wooden hearth is our daily opportunity to find shelter from the storm that is our unfortunate secular preoccupation with life. Maybe here we can find our peace and happiness. And, if there is a little path or window or door that leads our vision into that garden of Nature just outside our Tree, then let us make that place our sanctuary, too. And let us honor wood in its presence.

Perhaps Hermann Hesse says it best when we find ourselves wandering, our soul lost, amidst the trials and travails of life:

When we are stricken and cannot bear our lives any longer, then a tree has something to say to us: Be still! Be still! Look at me! Life is not easy, life is not difficult. Those are childish thoughts. Let God speak within you, and your thoughts will grow silent. You are anxious because your path leads away from mother and home. But every step and every day lead you back again to the mother. Home is neither here nor there. Home is within you, or home is nowhere at all . . . Whoever has learned how to listen to trees no longer wants to be a tree. He wants to be nothing except what he is. That is home. That is happiness.

Are *you* at home? Are *you* happy?

8

Garden Art

We seem to have lost contact with the earlier, more profound
functions of art, which have always had to do with personal
and collective empowerment, personal growth, communion
with this world, and the search for what lies
beneath and above this world.

—PETER LONDON,

No More Second Hand Art

The soul loves art and enchantment. A Sanctuary Garden offers its Keeper an open canvas for the thoughtful addition of well-crafted art of all types. Art is an honoring gesture, a timeless gift of celebration between human and Nature. Be it playful, sacred, thought-provoking, or sentimental, garden art expands on and amplifies the mood of its setting. And, when well-chosen, it can be one of your best allies in honing a very particular mood or eliciting a certain response.

Five or six years ago, I received a call from my successor as President of the Lane County Master Gardener Association asking me to make good on my promise to do a program on garden art. I had to tell Jackie that I had never made such a promise, and that I knew nothing whatsoever about the subject. She was gracious even when I declined her request. After I hung up the phone, however, I began to think about it, realizing several points. Although it was true that I had never studied or researched garden art, Forrest and I had intuitively been integrating it into our own garden (and home) for years.

My college degree and subsequent training were in fine arts, giving me at least a little credibility—and perhaps I had misinterpreted what Jackie had in mind. I was assuming that the art she referred to was the Renaissance style common in English castle and estate gardens. You know—bigger-than-life-size Venus statues, fair young maidens with birds in their hair or carrying basins of water, plump cherubs, and the like. That type of art, while nice in those settings, does not quite seem to fit in the average garden.

Then a brave thought occurred to me: What if I presented a different perspective on art in the garden—a kind of do-it-yourself art that any gardener could feel comfortable with? This concept would allow plenty of room for an individual's "artistic license," and seemed much more in keeping with the practical personality of most Master Gardeners, at least the ones I know. So I called

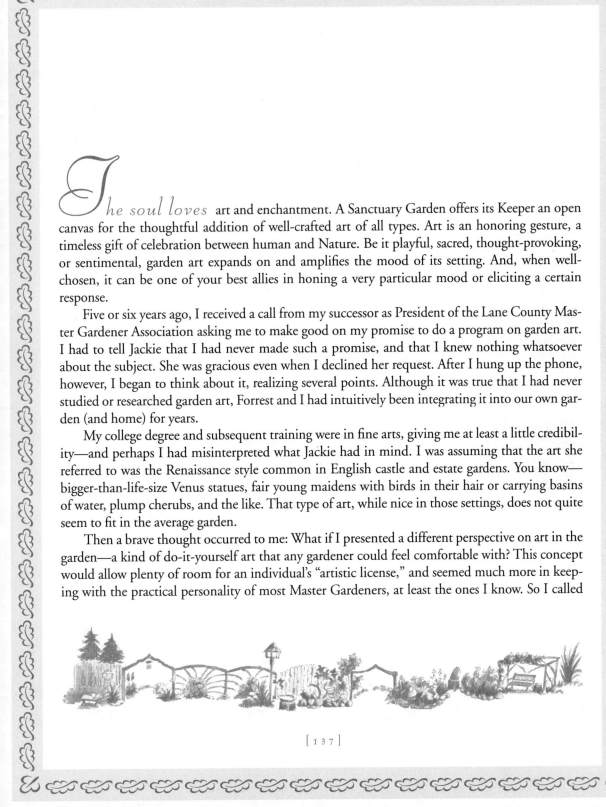

The Value of Garden Art

FOR THE SOUL

· It honors and celebrates life and the creative spirit.
· It symbolizes our human relationship to Nature.
· It serves as a catalyst for specific emotional responses.
· It stimulates humor, pathos, reflection, whimsy.
· It reflects the changing and evolving awareness of a culture.
· It deepens a sense of sacredness.

FOR THE GARDEN OR YARD

· It can enhance or complete the tone, mood, or feeling of intent in a given area.
· It fills in seasonal gaps in planting areas.
· Its location or design can be as temporary as desired.
· It is an opportunity to express humor or whimsy.
· It can enhance the effects of existing plants or the drama of a specific area.
· It allows the unique personality of the caretaker to be expressed.

Jackie back and told her that I had reconsidered, and would love to give the talk. She was enthusiastic about my approach. As I prepared for the talk over the next six months, suddenly I noticed garden art everywhere, took many color slides, visited gardens far and wide, and became very excited about the subject.

Little did I realize how instrumental Jackie's original request would be. It seems to have set me on a course that may well be a lifelong passion. So let's take a closer look at why you might want to consider integrating a bit of art into your sanctuary, on your terms, of course.

EXAMPLES OF GARDEN ART

I have fond memories of the many long walks Forrest and I took through our old neighborhood in town years ago. Inexperienced though we were, our little garden was an increasingly important part of our life. We were also curious about how others around us approached the craft, so we instituted the evening walks to see what others were doing. As we wandered the quaint side streets and also the substantial network of alleyways in South Eugene, we came across many gardens. Some were quite unremarkable and were quickly forgotten. While others were memorable because of a whimsical gate, a unique sculpture, or some other art piece charmingly placed among the plants.

We have often been captivated by how a mere postage stamp of a garden can be so expressive of its owner's personality. One small garden, for example, had a most unusual birdfeeder made entirely from tin cans and lids nailed together and mounted on a post. And on the unique bamboo and string pea trellises the owner had tied bright colored ribbons. These two additions made an otherwise rather small, ordinary garden become more special.

My friend Vicky offers another example. Art literally overflows from Vicky's tiny urban garden. She is a single mother on a very limited budget, but she doesn't let that prevent her from using her considerable artistic skills. Sitting at the garden entrance are two old chairs and a small table on which Vicky has painted lovely floral murals. She greets me at the gate wearing a hand-painted garden shirt. Even her rubber mud boots, which sit on the porch, are painted with bright flowers.

When Vicky walks her young son to school every day, she is constantly on the lookout for things she can use in her garden. She points to the entryway arch, reminiscent for her of the beloved childrens' book, *The Secret Garden*. The arch is woven from the neighborhood prunings of a climbing rose and a plum tree, as well as some delicate, curly willow branches knocked down in a winter storm. Scavenged bamboo poles serve as the support, and raffia ties it all together. This project required no tools, nails, or other materials, yet the resulting arch is beautiful and strong enough to support a variety of annual vines, including runner beans and sweet peas. Vicky also points out the Celtic wooden crosses hidden here and there among the beds, and a large crystal, both symbols that she believes exert a protective and purifying influence.

She prefers using natural or recycled materials in her garden and allowing her own innate creativity to gracefully blend art and plants together in her own special way. "I love this garden," Vicky says, "I look at it and it makes me happy. Before this my life was complete, utter hell, but now I'm being healed. This place is truly blessed."

The joy derived from this unique expression is, in my thinking, one of the primary purposes of garden art. It is a chance to dig deeper into the realm of imagination to express oneself separate from the homogeneity so rampant today. From clothing to furniture, cars to athletic shoes, nearly everything in modern countries seems to be mass-produced. Even today's gardening industry relies on mass-production of cheap tools, plastic pots, and an endless array of garden knick-nacks. Most of the plants we buy come from huge greenhouses, where they are grown in artificial mediums and conditions far from the reality of the backyard in which they will eventually end up.

Your personalized artistic expression may be as fleeting as a pretty shell or a vase of flowers set

on a stump in the shade, or as permanent as a rock wall or even a shrine or earth altar, as I'll discuss later. The important thing is that it comes from the heart. And, remember that garden art remains in place, if you choose, through all the seasons. Our simple stone statue of St. Francis is such a constant. Standing under a stately Douglas fir in our front meadow, whether in wind and rain, deep snow, or dappled summer sun, Francis is a comforting presence. Such sacred art tends to take on a life of its own over the years.

Let's consider a much more time-honored example to put garden art in a larger perspective. I read with great interest recently of the gardens at Pavlovsk, the beautiful estate near St. Petersburg, Russia. Here, from 1777 until her death in 1828, the grand duchess, and later tsarina, Maria Fyodorovna oversaw the meticulous transformation of 1800 acres into what writer Douglas Brenner calls "one of the greatest landscaped parks of its age—a masterpiece of 18th- and 19th-century style." ("The Tsarina's Garden," *Garden Design*, April/May 1996).

Now, Maria was no ordinary woman. She was an expert botanist with intimate knowledge of the soil and a great love of plants. She loved experimenting with trees, bulbs, roses, and seeds from around the world, to test their hardiness in the harsh Russian winters. She also developed a keen interest in garden art, of which there are many fine examples at Pavlovsk. Maria had 15 pavilions built, each with a different mood and purpose. Her favorite was the rose pavilion, which contained furniture, walls, and porcelain bearing images of the many, many varieties of roses carefully selected and tended in the surrounding gardens by Maria herself. The rose pavilion served as a sanctuary of sorts, and was also the scene for musicals, readings, and special celebrations. Its design serves as a perfect example of the partnership role played by plants and art, even if its scale is not one most of us can readily replicate.

When German forces were advancing in the early 1940's during the siege of Leningrad, many of Maria's fine bronze and marble statues were buried for safekeeping by loyal townspeople in hastily dug holes around the estate. Other magnificent pieces were successfully hidden as well. After the war, the sculptures were hoisted out of the ground and some 50,000 shrubs and trees were planted, again largely by volunteers. What was a charred wasteland of tree stumps, torched pavilions, and a ransacked palace, Brenner says, has now been remarkably restored by the courageous efforts of curators and townspeople. Pavlovsk is once again open to the public and stands as a great testimony to the love of one woman and, for that matter, an entire community, for the beauty of gardens and the art that ennobles them.

MAKING A PERSONAL STATEMENT

I shared Maria's story because I believe well-conceived, well-placed art of any style can stir peoples' passions and touch hearts in timeless, archetypal ways that are often hard to describe. We can learn from the great garden art of the ages, even while we find the way (within our means and tastes) to make our own contemporary statement, choosing or creating objects that best portray our inner world and our vision of life.

Thus, on the more personal scale, I want to underscore this key point about the use of art in the Sanctuary Garden. Because the soul is actively employed in the creation of such a garden, you have the opportunity to see beyond the art object itself to its inner meaning or significance for you. It matters not whether anyone else comprehends the significance of the art you select. It is chosen with your satisfaction in mind. But, your guests will feel, no doubt—each in their own way—the sincerity of your intention or even find their own meaning in your art. The soulfulness of your painting on the canvas that is your garden *is* tangible and accessible to others' understanding.

Our neighbor Linda's garden was full of interesting plants, but somehow the feeling was rather disjointed. She appeared to be a devoted yet frantic gardener who stuck things in here and there, with never enough time to hone some larger vision. After her husband died, her garden began to change. There was a long refinement stage. Winding paths were added, as were rock borders, specimen plants, and especially garden art. I don't pretend to understand the details of this transformation. I'm sure it involved much inner as well as outer work. What I do know is that these wonderful new touches allowed Linda to turn a patchy garden into an enviable sanctuary, with a tangible sense of unity of design.

As one matures in one's understanding of life, one's vision matures as well. Isn't it natural to

Guidelines for Art in the Sanctuary Garden

· Keep it simple at first. Begin by selecting just one or two pieces that really suit your personality and gardening style. Take your time, and be picky. You want your selections to feel just right. Ask yourself, "Will this piece really enhance the feeling of sanctuary in my garden?"

· Find the right place for your art. Place each piece of art meticulously, even if it's "just a rock" or a simple water bowl. Move it around until you are sure it's in its perfect place. View it from different perspectives.

· Let your own intuition be the judge. Don't ask anyone else's advice when selecting or placing garden art, as you're the one who will be living with it. Let your own intuition be your guide. Spouses may not always agree. In that case, you may have to cut a deal. ("You can buy that bench if I can . . .")

· It's okay to change your mind. You always reserve the right to change your mind about any art that's in your Sanctuary Garden. You may need to move it into a new location or perhaps get rid of it. Ask yourself, "Does this piece still fit in with what I'm trying to create?"

· Let your art create a mood. Art for your Sanctuary Garden can be subtle, funny,

expect that one's garden and the art within it would reflect this maturing? Again, this is the difference between an ordinary garden and the true Sanctuary Garden. In the words of a beloved Hindu chant, "He who knows, he knows; no one else knows." Indeed, there is a mysterious sense of timing to this inner knowing and its outer manifestations. We can seldom control it and can, at best, marvel at its subtleties.

Thus, one need not feel an artificial sense of urgency to incorporate garden art, or any other particular feature in one's sanctuary. This process should unfold naturally without being forced. You will know when some object you see speaks to your heart. It may come along when you least expect it—at a garage sale, as a gift from a dear friend, or in the woods. Once you open to the process, you may begin finding garden art in your travels and wanderings, whether nearby or far from home.

whimsical, thought-provoking, sacred . . . possessing whatever quality you want to evoke. Think of it as a mood enhancer or a key prop in a play that you are directing.

· Let some art come as gifts. If your budget is limited, let the more expensive items come to you as gifts. Over time, you'll be amazed at what presents itself. You can, of course, drop hints around Christmas, birthdays, and, especially, Mother's Day or Father's Day.

· Create your own folk art. Consider creating some of your own garden art, even if you don't consider yourself an artist. Call it *folk art*—that will give you plenty of latitude to experiment. Keep in mind that perfection is not the goal: self-expression is.

· Resist the museum look. Try not to acquire so much art that your garden starts looking more like a museum, unless that's the effect you really want. Understated beauty may be preferrable to overwhelming your garden visitors. If they can't find the plants for the art, you've gone too far.

· Keep your eyes open for the unexpected. Once you take an interest in garden art, it magically appears in the most unexpected places. If necessary, keep a list of measurements or specifications in your wallet or purse so that you know you'll get what you need. ("Gee, Honey, I thought this ten-foot Venus would fit perfectly on the deck . . .")

· Most of all, have fun selecting or creating garden art. Give yourself full creative license. And don't be surprised if your friends and neighbors get bitten by the garden-art bug as well. (The effects are definitely contagious.)

Secondhand stores, estate sales, and auctions are also fun places to discover fascinating treasures. It certainly doesn't have to be expensive to be just the right piece for you. You may just want to create your own art (see ideas in the preceding chart). It's the thought and interaction that is primary here. Like a dear, old friend with whom you've spent much time, your Sanctuary Garden (and every plant and art piece in it) will become more and more a part of you. In fact its presence will ever linger in the background of your mind. No doubt you'll appreciate more the sincere efforts of other Sanctuary Gardeners. You'll also find at every turn something new to inspire a deepening of your articulation of what sanctuary means to you.

SECULAR AND SACRED ART

The root and full practice of the arts lies in the recognition that art is power, an instrument of communion between the self and all that is important is sacred.

—*Peter London,*
No More Second Hand Art

QUEENIE TEAPOT

In my talks on art in the garden, I've often tried to distinguish between what I call *secular art* and sacred art. Secular art could be seen to be more casual, perhaps, without deep significance to its owner. I can't help it, but pink flamingos come to mind, as do the generic plastic garden chairs that grace so many yards and gardens across America. Certain themes, images, or products, when mass produced or repeated so freqently, may cease to have much impact on us when we view them, hence the label of secular or nonsacred.

I used to cite various examples of secular art here at Cortesia, but in all truthfulness, I feel unable to do that anymore. Why is that? Because every art object in our garden has been placed with tremendous consciousness and intent. This *doesn't* mean that we cannot be playful, whimsical, or downright humorous in our choices of art. We often are. But over time, each of those pieces has come to have its own deep significance to us, thus, they now fit into the category of sacred art. In other words, by its very nature the Sanctuary Garden will attract into its boundaries that which is sacred on some level. Playfulness can be sacred, can't it? Humor and irony are likewise aspects of the Divine, as much so as reverence or gratitude or hope. May all of these aspects or qualities be reflected in our own multifaceted character and in the visage of our garden.

"FAUCET FAIRY"

If you visited Cortesia, you would come upon Queenie Teapot, a very large ceramic teapot made by a dear friend, Angela. This art piece sits near our entrance, next to a small pool, and has been additionally colored with mosses and weathered by time. Part of the tiered lid has cracked off. But Queenie stands as a whimsical symbol of the Alice-in-Wonderland world where, of course, teapots talk. They entertain their guests with nonsensical stories even while they pour endless cups of tea, to everyone's delight.

Angela, a free-hearted young painter and potter in her final year of art school, introduced playfulness into our life here as no one else ever has. Her freeform pots are all over the garden, each a spontaneous gift from their creator. She once made me a walking staff decorated at the top with yarn and shells and tufts of her own hair. While she has since disappeared from our life, fully immersed in her own whimsical adventures around the world, Angela's spirit remains, reminding us to be less serious and more adventurous.

Beyond Queenie, up in the main garden, you would encounter another imaginative piece we call Faucet Fairy. She was a Mother's Day gift to me from Forrest and Sonji, who made her from a recycled bicycle fork and gears (the legs and body), an old water faucet (the head), and a red plastic scouring pad (symbolic of my red hair). Faucet Fairy is prominently placed in front of the first and most visible raised vegetable bed (more recently overrun with volunteer flowers). Forrest calls this type of art *silly art*. But don't underestimate the intent behind it. While stuffy gardeners might be a little nonplussed, Faucet Fairy never fails to make people smile, and she whispers to me when I work too hard, to lighten up and enjoy life.

CERAMIC WALL MURAL

Another interesting addition of silly art was inspired by a visit to a well-known regional art fair. In the garden art area, we saw fancifully painted bowling balls selling for $175. Forrest and I rolled our eyes at the price, and he whispered to me, "I can do better than that!" A week later, which happened to be my birthday, I returned home from doing errands to find bowling balls literally all over the garden. They were mounted on pedestals, placed in color-coordinated flower beds, and even upended on two-foot lengths of steel rebar as hose-guards along garden paths. (Forrest later confessed that he went to a local secondhand store and, to their delight, bought every last bowling ball they had.) We're still waiting to see whether or not this is the beginning of a new nationwide trend.

Near the Meditation Garden, where a bench affords the visitor a long view across a grassy commons, there is a wooden wall to the right on which hangs the light-hearted ceramic creations of our daughter, Sonji; son, Oceah; and my efforts at a clay-sculpture class. All of the items are creatures of the ocean and seashore, and they usually generate an appreciative smile and chuckle. Another outgrowth of our class are the clay masks seen around the garden, subtly hanging from a limb or sitting by a rock.

Can you see how playful and fun these various art projects can be? And yet they are certainly not devoid of deeper meaning. That is the nature of art, for it affects each of us differently. I love what the great American conservationist Aldo Leopold says: "Our ability to perceive quality in nature begins, as in art, with the pretty. It expands through successive stages of the beautiful to values as yet uncaptured by language."

In our choices of art for our Sanctuary Garden, we can endeavor to move beyond what is simply cute or pretty or popular to a place that calls up real feeling, whether that be humor, pathos, peace, or celebration. In attuning to or eliciting a more soulful response, we will have accomplished in some way the very goal of sacred art throughout time: to draw us closer to spirit.

I want to describe a few of the other pieces of garden art at Cortesia, so that you have a sense of the breadth of possibilities. Each has its own story of how it came to be in our garden. In fact I like to imagine that there are amazing things out there even now that were created just for Cortesia and merely await our discovery at the right moment. For example, we are searching for just the right laughing Ho Ti to place near the garden entrance. We don't know when will we find one, but it's only a matter of time . . .

Forrest mentioned earlier the large white calcite crystal given to us by our friend Barbara. It has such a powerful presence that I am stunned whenever I pass it. I feel that it is truly alive. Near it stands an intricately detailed, ivory-colored angel with the sweetest smile. I saw her in a local shop. Although my budget did not allow me to purchase her, I was convinced that she was ours. That evening we received a phone call from Forrest's mother in Missouri saying she was sending us a Christmas check early, with which to buy something very special for ourselves. The amount of the check exactly matched the cost of the angel.

Of course, there are any number of birdhouses here, many of them beautifully crafted by artists with a flair for the unusual. We always make sure when purchasing such a nesting box, that it has the right size of entrance hole (not too large) and that it allows easy access for cleaning at the end of each season. Imagine having a real art piece that some happy bird couple actually moves into to raise a family.

One of the more sensitive and creative expressions of Sanctuary Garden art are those pieces that celebrate the natural elements and forces of Nature. The words of William Shakespeare, in *The Winter's Tale,* reminds us that, "So, over that art/which you say adds to nature, is an art/That nature makes." Forrest and I both have received incredible satisfaction from our efforts at showcasing Nature's natural artistry. I, for example, have a fondness for discovering uniquely contorted driftwood at the seashore. We finally gathered a few of the more expressive pieces I've brought home and tilted them upright in the ground at a particular spot along the path near the entrance.

Another natural wooden art piece—a burl-contorted slab of bark, about two feet by four— was given to us by a one-time visitor. The woman travelled all the way from Colorado just to come

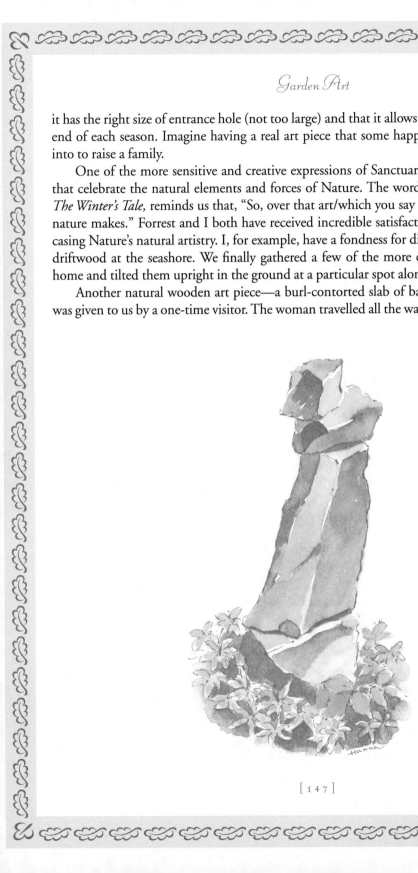

Garden Art Projects You Can Do Yourself

- Get a secondhand wooden chair, stool, or end table and repaint it (using enamel paint) in bright floral patterns, stripes, or whatever suits your fancy. Color coordinate your artpiece with a flower bed and set it near it or on your patio or deck. A great kid's project, too.
- Make your own ceramic sculptures (you may need to take a class). You can make masks, animals, simple water bowls, birdhouses, among many other objects to place around your garden or yard. Another fun kid's project.
- Rummage through a local secondhand store for unique or off-beat items. Yes, you might even find a worthy art project by painting an old bowling ball. Don't rule out an old, cheap picture, perhaps of a floral or pastoral scene, that could be hung outside on a wooden fence.
- Place shallow saucers or bowls in various elevated places (stumps, flat rocks, etc.) around the garden. Add a few stones as sunning islands for butterflies, dragonflies, and others.
- Make mobiles out of shells or small rocks with holes in them, letting them hang down from arches, trellises, or tree branches.
- Collect driftwood, branches, stumps or rocks that have unique personalities, texture, and color. Place them upright, stack them, or do other creative things with them.

to Cortesia to register herself as a sanctuary with our Cortesia Sanctuary Project. So stunned by the setting and her sense of its sacredness, she told Forrest that she had been carrying this natural wooden "shield" with her for over twelve years, her sojourn starting in Michigan and leading her all over the United States. It was here at Cortesia, however, that she believed the bark was meant to stay. And so it has, sitting like a suspended backrest behind Forrest's rough hewn wood slab bench near the entrance.

All of the natural art pieces are placed so subtly that they almost blend in with the overall drama of our garden's setting. In fact, repeat visitors often comment that they discovered items or features overlooked in previous excursions to Cortesia. One such item, however, that is rarely missed is the magic of the wind. This natural force, too, is elevated to the level of art here in our gardens. We have planted numerous ornamental grasses, for example, to specifically highlight the effect of wind through their panicles. One would only desire to sit and listen to the oceanic roar of

- On masonite, canvas, a wooden panel, or even an old bamboo blind paint a garden mural to mount on a bare fence or wall.
- Hang wind chimes in those parts of the garden that receive the most breeze. Try making your own tinkling chimes out of found metal such as old silverware, metal piping, bicycle sprockets, or even thick, resonating pieces of wood (they clatter more than ring) or thin slabs of sliced rock.
- Build a unique birdhouse with lots of personality. First, however, find out the necessary dimensions of the interior and the correct height and size of the entrance hole. Otherwise, no birds (or the wrong kind of bird) will find it safe or usable.
- Create one or more earth altars using found objects from Nature, such as stones, crystals, shells, bones, wood, leaves, seeds, blossoms, etc. The altar itself can be a simple stump, large flat-topped rock, or even a small table.
- Find an old, funky garden chair that is no longer useful for sitting. Immortalize it by placing it in a wildflower bed, at the back of a border, or amongst the shrubs.
- Build a simple bench using recycled wood, stumps, curved fallen branches and the like.
- When you are ready, create a shrine area that is a bit separate from the rest of the yard or garden. Make it special and dedicate it in a simple ceremony you share with friends.

"om" as the wind blows through the towering firs of our Cortesian woods. Forrest, as the musician he is, has also created an opportunity for one to dive into the blissful and soulful relaxing sounds of the wind through numerous carefully selected and placed wind chimes.

I could go on and on, but you get the idea. The sky is the limit. Give your soul the free range of expression to introduce well-conceived art that is uniquely suited to your personality and that of your garden. Be daring. Be sincere. And as you evolve in this process, you may want to consider creating what we call an *earth altar* or a *shrine*. Let me share some thoughts with you about these purely spiritual features which can elevate the true feeling of sanctuary in your yard or garden.

EARTH ALTARS

It is ironic that our very concept of art, and what is required to make it, dooms most would-be artists to frustration and modest results . . . The correlate of "art as beauty" is "art as meaning." The correlate of a prepared hand and eye is a prepared heart, mind, and spirit. The correlate of the formulas of good design is the absence of any formula, where imagination serves as a better guide than memory, and where courage fuels the journey from the known to the unknown.

— Peter London,
No More Second Hand Art

One of the deepest expressions of art in the garden, we feel, can come in the form of what we call *earth altars.* Defined primarily on the basis of the intention behind them, earth altars are as varied as the personalities of their creators, yet they share one thing in common. They are created as an act of reverence and gratitude—to God, Nature, and the Spirit within all living things. Earth altars can be placed directly on the soil, on a stump or small table, in a lush bed of moss, amongst the flowers, at the base of a tree. They act as a spiritual focal point of sorts and are often most effective if done very simply. A single statue, a few contrasting rocks or polished stones, a grouping of shells, an artful piece of driftwood, a flower floating in a basin of water. The possibilities are endless.

Sometimes, earth altars are created spontaneously when one is visiting some beautiful place in Nature. Or, perhaps, the urge rises up out of an intense emotional experience. Some years ago, my father died while I was up in the mountains for a few days. By the time I returned, it was too late to attend the funeral, which was thousands of miles away. So I hiked up to the most sacred place I knew of close at hand, and performed my own funeral ritual. Part of this involved creating an earth altar on a beautiful mossy rock using found objects from the forest clearing and a small photograph of my father. I sang, recited poetry, and, most important, symbolically released my father to God. It was a deeply comforting experience, which I was glad I did alone. It allowed me to come to a real sense of completion with my father, even while I continue to remember and value his outstanding qualities and the lessons I learned from him.

Forrest and I have created earth altars on beaches, mountaintops, in shady forest glens, wherever the spirit moves us. Once, our family spent an entire afternoon in ninety-plus-degree weather erecting rock towers in a fast-flowing mountain stream. We called them the *Shikan Towers,* a tribute to a Zen form of mindfulness given to a particular task. It takes fortitude, believe me, to keep one's footing in such a cold, fast stream and to balance the rocks carefully enough that they don't topple, but we had a superb time doing it.

Often, earth altars such as these are created in places we never return to, but that is not important. The power is in the act of creating and, again, in the clarity of the intention behind the act. If others come upon your creation, wonderful. They may or may not perceive its significance. But *you* will be changed. And if you place earth altars in your garden and visit them often, you will be even more deeply changed. Through the sacred associations you establish there and continue to cultivate over time, I believe you will empower yourself on the soul level in ways you would not even guess. The sheer unconditionality of such an act becomes a kind of blessing in and of itself.

CREATING A SHRINE

Shrines make a spirit palpably present; they celebrate rather than explain and generate intimacy between the human and the more than human . . . . A shrine transfers the holiness of faith and whatever spirit is captured by sacred imagination to a particular place for memory and honor.

—*Thomas Moore,*
The Re-enchantment of Everyday Life

An earth altar conceived of, and created on, a larger and more permanent scale could be called a *shrine*. A Sanctuary Garden is as worthy a place as any to erect a shrine, but such an act deserves careful consideration. There is a rich legacy of shrines spread across this earth, representative of nearly every culture in history. The word *shrine* comes from the Latin *scrinium,* a box or container, and the idea of shrine, as Thomas Moore says, "lies at the very heart of the religious impulse. It is also a primary means of sustaining an enchanted world." You may have seen, for example, one of the Native American sites with various petroglyphs honoring the Great Spirit, certain forces in Nature, or depicting various aspects of daily life. Seeing such ancient art, preserved over all these centuries, is a powerful way to experience the sacredness of life as seen through the unknown eyes of our ancestors from the past.

I was deeply moved, during my first trip to Hawaii two years ago, to have the privilege of visiting several *heiaus*. A *heiau* is an ancient Hawaiian temple—a place of worship, offering, and/or sacrifice. The sheer age of these sacred sites impressed me greatly, but the fact that these shrines are still actively used by Hawaiians today means even more to me. Although all that remains in most cases are remnants of the massive stone foundations, the power of these sites is immediately apparent.

In his book, *Ancient Sites of O'ahu,* author Van James describes the original purpose of such sacred sites: "With an intense and immediate experience of the forces in nature and an intuitive relationship with their gods, the ancient Hawaiians looked to the heiau and their kahuna (priest) for order, understanding, and guidance in the ways of the universe." At the *heiaus,* in addition to seeking guidance in practical everyday matters of all sorts, the *kahuna* (ruler) and commoners showed their gratitude and reverence by presenting offerings of flowers, food, and other objects.

My mother and I visited a *heiau* on the Na Pali coast of the island of Kauai, which we only discovered by accident as we followed a steep, rocky trail up the mountainside. We were moved to see, amidst the temple ruins, a crude stone altar covered with fresh offerings of food, herbs, and flowers. As I sat in silence and meditation near the altar and later gazed out upon the incredible tropical paradise spread out far below, I could really feel the centuries of devotion seeping into me and changing me deeply.

At Pu'uhonua O Honaunau, or "Place of Refuge," on the Kona side of the Big Island, I experienced perhaps the deepest sense of sanctuary that I have ever felt. Created at least five-hundred years ago, Place of Refuge served as a sanctuary for women and children, defeated warriors, criminals, and those who had in some way broken the sacred laws or *kapu.* In those days, the *kapu* was so strict that even small infractions were punishable by death. But, if a violator could somehow escape his pursuers and make his way, by land or water, into the boundaries of this most sacred of *heiaus,* he was granted instant forgiveness. After a short period of prayer and fasting, he was ceremoniously purified by the *kahuna* and then set free. When he returned home, his life was begun anew with no further stigma attached to his previous wrong actions.

Not only does this concept have profound implications in any age, but imagine the buildup of energy in a place that has symbolized forgiveness for hundreds of years. (Not to mention that this was also the original burial place of thirteen revered Hawaiian kings.) It wasn't just the physical power of the place, with its massive stone walls, giant wooden totems, authentically replicated structures, and pristine beach. It was the pure feeling there that permeated my soul on the deepest level. Thomas Moore tells us, "The spirit of a place or many other kinds of spirit can be focused into a shrine, where we can sense its intensity and recognize its personality." Indeed, I have rarely felt such peace and tranquility as I experienced at Place of Refuge. I felt that I was literally breathing in the gratitude and forgiveness of centuries of pilgrims. Truly, it convinced me more than any other experience in my life of the power and nobility of sanctuary and the importance of creating it in a tangible way for myself and others, and as a permanent legacy to the Earth.

We began the creation of our own shrine not long after my return from Hawaii. I had already planted a number of ornamental grasses there two years earlier, and the dry creek bed which begins its flow down from the Shrine into the main garden was flanked by a huge trellised kiwi vine to the north and trellised grape vines to the south. It wasn't until Forrest built a prominent cedarwood arch that we began to recognize the full impact of what we were creating.

Rising up above the foliage at the highest point of our property, the triple arch had an immediate transformative effect on the entire garden. But it was Hanna, coming one day to paint, who first called it a shrine. She said the arch reminded her of the shrines of Japan. On New Year's Day there, she explained, it was customary for every Japanese citizen to make a pilgrimage to their favorite shrine. There, each would make an offering of money, and pray for good health and happiness for themselves and their family during the coming year. As the priest chanted a mantra, each visitor would ring a large bell and perhaps light a candle. Hanna asked if she could make a pilgrimage to our shrine on January 1st. We were very honored. Following her prayer ritual we shared in a traditional Japanese feast that Hanna had lovingly prepared. After that, we, too, began to treat the shrine as a sacred place.

In his essay, "The Shrine of the Mountain and the Waters," Oregon architect Tom Bender writes movingly about the purpose of shrines. "What shrines show us is what we hold sacred, what we value so greatly as to hold inviolate. They have made visible the depth of meaning that a place or person has. They have shown us the empowerment of our connection with the rest of nature and the breath of life that infuses it."

Tom describes the simple yet honored shrines that line the roadsides of India, Mexico, Africa, and elsewhere. We have also seen friends' photographs of these shrines in Japan and Nepal. They are an important part of daily life in many cultures. Perhaps it is time for Americans to begin cultivating such a reverent awareness in their own lives without shame or embarassment.

Tom continues, "When the spiritual core of a religion is clear and strong in a society, conventions exist for the making of a shrine. At times when we are reforging the spiritual dimensions of our lives, we have also to fashion anew the expression of that spiritual nature. This is particularly true when we want a place to be accessible to all people without blockage by religious symbolism which is adverse to them."

Talking about his own circle of friends creating a double shrine on top a mountain and at the headwaters of the river at its base, Tom says: "We've gone to the shrines (we created) at sunrise, in full moon, in fog, rain, and snow. From them we've watched the moon rise over the bay in full eclipse, and seen a comet in the night sky. We've gone there alone, and together; for comfort and inspiration and thanksgiving. With each visit, the gift that they have given us increases and deepens, and what they represent to us becomes more encompassing."

The Shrine at Cortesia is still young, but already it is a very special place. Locating it at the top and back of the garden makes it the culmination, in a sense, of the experience of Cortesia gardens because usually it is the last place visitors come to. If desired, one can look out upon the sweeping view down the slope of the garden and across to the impressive forest beyond. (Some of this will be obscured when the grapes and other newer vines fill out their trellises.) But one could literally cocoon oneself away, hidden from the world if they choose, sitting under the cool leafy canopy of the massive kiwi vines. This notion to cocoon oneself is extended to the entering visitor, for sitting perched on a decaying stump of wood is a smooth rounded stone inscribed with one word: *Surrender*. Indeed, a shrine is an ideal place for metamorphosis.

The elegant, oversized birdbath, positioned at the top of the dry creek bed, is a focal point in The Shrine. It symbolizes, via water, that fount of Spirit and Life from which our souls emerge. At the back of this birdbath, framing the large wooden altar like hands, is an espaliered apple tree (with four varieties) symbolizing the archetypal Tree of Life or Knowledge. Placed conspicuously near these icons are Forrest's handmade bench and a lovely bentwood throne chair. The large altar, with its accompanying statue and objects, receives the pilgrims' offerings, if they wish to leave one. And, all around, hanging from the various trellises, are the most wonderful wind chimes, which ring in the faintest breeze. Their combined sound is hauntingly beautiful. Forrest is passionate about reminding the visitor that the "breath of God" is all about us. These chimes increase one's desire to surrender to this thought. We plan to have small prayer flags available for guests, perhaps to write on and hang from one of the overhead trellises. Or, they may choose to place a rock upon the large cairn nearby as an enduring symbol of the energy they bring and give to the shrine. These types of interactive opportunities empower the site even more, we feel, and make a visitor feel connected to the power of the place.

As you can see, garden art plays a significant role in the shrine, certainly equal to the ornamental grasses that surround it, blowing majestically in the breeze. We have delighted in the creation of such a magical and holy setting, and those who come there seem to feel its healing qualities. Like the ancient wayside shrines in the Far East, we feel the sacred energy slowly accumulating here—as a permanent legacy to this land and whoever comes after us. It is good, at times, to imagine our humble role within the lineage of the history of a place and yet to behave as if our contribution really matters, which it does. In this way we empower ourselves and others to envision the noblest of futures, wherein we each become like a delicate wind chime, ringing in the gentle breeze of the sweet breath of Spirit.

As the Keeper of the Art and Creative Beauty of our sanctuary, may we, in conclusion, find passion and humility in these words of Thomas Moore: "Loss of soul is an ever-present danger for all of us; we need numerous ways of sheltering the soul and housing spirits so that they will not disappear from loss of memory or sheer evaporation in the plethora of things and events that blow through our lives. All that is required is the homely art of keeping and caring, an art available to anyone who takes the time and gives attention to the spirits that preserve natural religion—life-giving piety in a world too often given to impieties and forgetfulness."

Blessed be.

9

Habitat for Wildlife

Until he extends the circle of his compassion
to all living things, man will not himself find peace.

ALBERT SCHWEITZER

There once was a selfish gardener, who was determined to keep all the bounty of his garden to himself. He especially did all he could to keep the animals and insects away. "Pests, all of them!" he scoffed. "Why, the birds come and eat all my precious berries and fruit, and they leave their droppings all around the grounds. And the bees pester me—I can't even walk around without fear of getting stung. And I don't trust caterpillars—who knows what they'll eat, maybe my tomatoes or prized dahlias. And the frogs keep me awake at night with their bellowing. And the moles and gophers destroy my lawn. And I certainly have never seen a good bug, ever! And God help a neighbor's cat or dog who gets in! Undesirables, all of them!" the selfish gardener scowled.

And for these reasons, the gardener set traps, sprayed insecticide, squished bugs between his fingers, shot BBs at the birds, and secured a very tight fenceline to keep other animals out. His garden was indeed lovely but very quiet. Nothing moved but the slight rustle of wind through the plants.

One day, the gardener fell sick and had to be hospitalized. He frantically worried who was going to keep the undesirables out of his garden. Then, he closed his eyes in sleep and all the animals and insects of the world came to his bedside. In a dream, he looked into each of their eyes, and saw only the reflection of his prone body. They nestled in close to him, but did not judge the poor man. They just wanted to see him, touch him, smell him, lick him. They simply wanted to know why he was the way he was. He looked rather harmless just lying there. So, they began to pray for his recovery. In his dream, the patient lay very still, taking in the animals' compassion, and this is what sparked a response in his heart.

"A miracle!" The doctors proclaimed when the old gardener suddenly awoke from his coma. In a day's time he went home with a change of heart, and he had a plan. He put on his finest clothes and hat and rushed out into the very center of his garden. He raised his hands up high in a

gesture for all to come, and all the animals and insects and wildlife in his area gathered along the fence. But now none of them dared enter for fear of the new scarecrow they saw standing in the middle of the garden.

Albert Schweitzer states: "Affirmation of life is the spiritual act by which man ceases to live unreflectively and begins to devote himself to his life with reverence in order to raise it to its true value. To affirm life is to deepen, to make more inward, and to exalt the will to live."

It is fitting to share that the seventh design element of a Sanctuary Garden is to affirm the sacredness of all those beings who find haven within a yard or garden. If we are truly our garden's Keeper, then we must reflectively extend our circle of compassion to all species without judgement. Similarly, in the larger gardens of cultures, communities, families, neighborhoods, and natural environments, we should want to embrace the uniqueness and diversity of life that abounds around us on this planet.

A Sanctuary Garden is a microcosm of how we view and treat the world. This is not to say that certain "undesirables" may not visit our sacred outdoor setting and shake things up a little too much for our liking. But, as our garden's Keeper, we must first enter the garden ourself with an attitude of reverence, knowing that if we are armed for a fight to control or cajole the many species who visit or dwell within, *we* in fact may be the biggest pest of all.

Throughout each of the seven design elements discussed in this book, Tricia and I have emphasized the necessity to see ourselves not just as gardeners but as co-creative partners with Nature. This mode of stewardship and trusteeship asks us to be the Keeper of the Spirit of our garden, as this Spirit is experienced to be the collective consciousness of all species and life forms in the garden. Hildegard von Bingen reminds us, "It is God whom human beings know in every creature." Clearly, when we build into our garden design due consideration for wildlife, be they large, small or miniscule, we are embracing God in many forms. As the ancient *Bhagavadgita* of India proclaims: "We bow to all beings with great reverence in the thought and knowledge that God enters into them through fractioning Himself as living creatures." This belief is also echoed by St. Paul in the Christian Bible, when he speaks of "one God who is Father of all, over all, through all and within all" (Eph. 4:6). The Trappist monk Thomas Merton expressed a similar perception: "We are living in a world that is absolutely transparent and God is shining through it all the time. God manifests Himself everywhere, in everything—in people and in things and in nature and in events . . . The only thing is we don't see it . . . I have no program for this seeing. It is only given. But the gate of heaven is everywhere."

Yes, the gate of heaven *can* be the very entrance to that place of refuge in our yard or garden. The attitude in which we enter colors our whole perception of the life that abounds within. Our garden *ceases* to be a sanctuary for a reverent philosophy if we enter it to practice extermination and uninformed control over various species based on fear. It *grows* as a place of refuge if we are

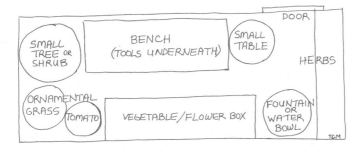

EVEN A BALCONY CAN BE A SANCTUARY GARDEN !
(BE SURE TO INCLUDE HANGING BASKETS WITH
FUSHIAS + RED FLOWERS FOR HUMMINGBIRDS
AND PERHAPS A BIRDFEEDER AND WINDCHIME)

willing to withhold judgment long enough to watch and understand the dynamics of its creatures.

We deepen as our garden's Keeper when we learn what is right for the overall well-being of our haven, at the same time we are not so rigid in our expectations. We learn, for example, to intervene on behalf of plant and animal life when clearly the garden environment appears out of balance. Yet, we also learn to respect the important ecological law of diversity, knowing that a rich, diverse, natural environment has its own checks and balances to naturally control the growth of its vegetal and animal species.

Without question, the Cortesian philosophy of reverence for life is most put to the test when creating a haven for wildlife. In no other design feature are we, as stewards of Nature, more in need of seeing life through the eyes and intent of another species.

Some of our own family's most heartwarming (and often humorous) stories at Cortesia center around our relationship to the many other species who visit or dwell within our gardens, woods, and meadows. We have witnessed birth, vibrant life, and death as but the cycle of seasonal life. We have learned deeper compassion at the feet of God's lovely creatures, large and small. We have found our role as but one species in God's sacred web. Let us share a few of our stories and thoughts as we give some practical ideas on how to create and sustain a hospitable habitat in your outdoor place of refuge. One of our most enduring experiences is with a frail calf named Sparky, as Tricia shares with us.

SPARKY'S GIFT

We received an interesting phone call from our neighbor one evening, as we were making dinner. She was asking us to care for her two-month old calf for ten days while she went camping. "But we're vegetarians," Forrest protested when I told him. "We don't want a cow in our front meadow." (He was cooking tofu for dinner at the time.) Nevertheless, we agreed, although somewhat reluctantly.

So the next morning our neighbor arrived with the little calf in the front seat of her station wagon. It was obviously not well. Sparky, as we came to call her, had been rejected by her mother shortly after birth. Denied the milk and the nurturing she so needed, she became weak and listless. In fact she clearly would have died had not Lynn brought her home from her mother's nearby farm and fed her a bottle morning and night for two months. So, this was the task I was inheriting for ten days, or so it seemed.

Sparky could barely walk. Her little front legs were malformed, with big lumps at the joints. She hobbled painfully or, more preferably, lay down. We kept her, untied, in the little meadow in front of our house. (She couldn't have gone anywhere even if she wanted too.) At feeding times, she had little interest in the large bottle of milk that I warmed and offered her. Suckling was another skill she was weak in, so most of the time she only drank half the bottle. We tried to feed her some supplementary grain, but she didn't know how to chew very well either. Forrest tried working her jaw as I spoonfed the grain into her mouth, but it didn't work.

Never having had a cow before, I lacked certain skills and knowledge. I called the local feed store for advice, but I really had no choice other than to proceed intuitively, using whatever alternative methods I could create. I decided to try several things. First, I added one of my Flower Essence blends (Woundedness Recovery) to Sparky's milk and water. Then I began doing *Reiki* on her at feeding times and massaging and brushing her as well. I talked to her in a soft, soothing voice, as if she were a little child. I told her how much I loved her and that God loved her too, and would make sure she was always cared for.

After a week or so, Sparky began to respond. She was much less afraid of me and her appetite was improving. She seemed to love wandering in the meadow and even began grazing. By the time our neighbors returned from their vacation, she was making enough progress that I didn't want to give her back right away. I begged for another week with her. When that week was over, I asked for another, and another. (Was I attached, or what?)

Sparky wandered far enough now during her daily grazing that we had to tie her up. She didn't like this, and often she got the rope tangled in the ferns or bushes or around her legs. Eventually, I decided to let her wander freely, grazing wherever she chose. I trusted that she would be okay. She began to spend more and more time in the woods during the day, and finding her at feeding time was often difficult. But, all in all, she seemed stronger and happier with her freedom, so it was worth it.

I learned a new *Reiki* technique several months after Sparky's arrival. I tried it on her one evening. The next morning, for the first time, she came up to the porch at feeding time and mooed loudly for me to come. She had never before made a sound. I was stunned. I considered it no insignificant thing that Sparky had at last found her voice. After that, she came to the porch each morning and evening for meals, and other times as well if she wanted to see me. We became closer than ever. At night Sparky would sometimes sleep near me in the woods near the house. And I continued daily with the flower essences, *Reiki,* massage, and brushing, and our long conversations about life.

While she never grew in height, Sparky did grow in girth and in spirit. Clearly, she was very small for her age. I knew she was probably not developing normally and I worried that she was lonely for other cows, but she seemed strangely content. My dear friend from college days, Daniel, unexpectedly came to visit one day. He is a doctor and cattle rancher in the California Sierras. He was amazed by Sparky. In spite of her congenital problems, she seemed to be thriving in my care. He said he'd never before seen a cow like her, and especially one who so loved the woods. He told me to watch for increasing signs of contentment that would indicate her will and ability to overcome her physical limitations. And this is exactly what I began to see. Now and then her lame little legs would break into a run or she would literally jump up in the air and click her heels together. I figured that she must be happy.

Over time, Sparky began to wander so far each day that she discovered the road and our neighbor's garden. Since we lacked any fences, we were forced to start tying her up again. She was very upset. I realized her days with us were numbered. I began more seriously to wean her off the bottle and to introduce more hay into her diet, lessening the grain. Soon we would need to take her back to the farm of her birth. I was devastated at the thought of losing her, but it seemed inevitable.

Finally, on December 21st, Winter Solstice, the weaning process complete, we loaded Sparky into a trailer and drove the fifteen miles to the farm. I cried all the way there, but she held her head up high as if she knew that going home was the right thing to do. When we arrived she literally leapt out of the trailer. The apparent leader of the herd saw her from across the field and approached with a loud moo. She sniffed Sparky, rubbed noses with her, and gave the approval for the others to come. It was a moving scene, no pun intended. All the cows mooed loudly. Than, one by one, they each approached Sparky and touched noses. Soon she was surrounded and welcomed back into the herd. The youngest of the calves of her age (her twin sister?) seemed particularly interested in her. She was twice the size of Sparky. I left grief-stricken yet knowing that her reentry was a success.

I never saw Sparky again. My neighbors reported that she was doing well but, two months later, Sparky was found dead following a deep snow, her exact cause of death unknown. She died during the same week that my friend Harriet was killed in India. I like to imagine that she died peacefully in the sweet white stillness of the first and last snow she would ever see, wiser in her diminutive body than we humans could ever know.

I think of Sparky often, and of the sanctuary we were able to provide for her here during her time of need. I wanted to make up, in some small yet symbolic way, for the incredible mistreatment of cows all over the world. But, beyond this, through the power of our healing experience with Sparky, we have come to envision more than ever the sanctuary for all creatures that Cortesia is and must be.

Mother Theresa once said, "We cannot do great things in life; we can only do small things with great love." I share Sparky's story to inspire you to find your own way to love the creatures of this Earth more deeply, with a great love from your heart. There are so many small ways that we can help just in our own backyard: nesting boxes, birdfeeders, ponds and birdbaths, planting native trees and shrubs that provide fruit, nuts, berries, and shelter for birds and others.

Above all, if we can accept on some level that creatures large, small, and microscopic have their own nobility of purpose, their own rightful role to play in this earthly drama, we need never again question the right of any being to live their life freely, unhampered by ignorant or selfish human behaviors. To enhance life for all who come there—this should be the clear intent behind every Sanctuary Garden. In living this simple yet profound truth, we surely become part of the vast and sacred web of Nature that Forrest so eloquently describes. Indeed, it may be said that it is our duty to be a loving Keeper of the Web of Life in our places of refuge. For, to honor and consciously experience the group soul of this Earth Sanctuary is to know God which, I believe, is our highest purpose in life.

UNBOUNDED BY FENCE OR DESIRE

Unlike most rural properties we come across in our excursions, the twenty-two acres of Cortesia Sanctuary is unfenced. In part, this reflects Tricia's and my perceived sense of duty in life. Ours is to tear down those attitudinal fences that separate people from people and people from Nature. If we create little personal sanctuaries in our backyards, we run the risk of walling in our compassion toward the larger gardens of our communities, cultures, natural environments, and the like; that is, we risk becoming too selfish in our desire to bring more joy, beauty, hope and peace into *our* lives alone. We need to find ways to give these gifts of sanctuary *back* to the world.

Gautama Buddha advised, "The key to a new civilization is the spirit of *maitri*, compassionate kinship with all creatures." He also suggested that "Friendship toward all creatures is the true religion." These truths live at Cortesia in both our reverent philosophy and practice. They live in the memory of Sparky and many other creatures. When we honor the creatures who live in and visit our yards and gardens, we are in a small way giving the gift of sanctuary back to the world. We are thinking less of ourselves.

Often, who better than a child to remind us of such philanthropy of heart? Our daughter Sonji's room is filled with play animals (it's hard to say "stuffed animals"), each of whom has a name and special personality. Her room is their sanctuary, but her heart is the larger chamber of compassion. One day, for example, Sonji discovered a newborn mouse around the piano, obviously far removed from its mother. She mothered Basil as best she could for three days before he died. She was devastated, but honored Basil with a ceremony and a private funeral, complete with a lovely headstone. Sonji's compassion for creatures amazes me. Unafraid, she will move spiders to more secure living quarters, rescue birds who have accidentally hit the window, and even assist unwanted ants from the house. Comedian Bob Hope once said "Those who lack charity of the heart have the worst form of heart disease." Sonji's heart is very strong and alive with charity.

At the beginning of this book, we shared how the first icon we brought to Cortesia was a statue of St. Francis, who sits facing the house in the front meadow. I am especially drawn to St. Francis, not only for his unspoken Cortesian philosophy for life, but because he too was a man of words, in poetry and song, as I am myself. One of Francis's most revered contributions is his *Canticle of the Creatures,* also known as *The Canticle of Brother Sun and Sister Moon.* St. Francis composed this canticle in 1225, shortly before his death, in the garden of his resurrected church, San Damiano. Francis is reported to have said about this piece, "For His (God's) praise, I wish to compose a new hymn about the Lord's creatures, of which we make daily use, without which we cannot live, and with which the human race greatly offends its Creator."

Think of your outdoor place of refuge as a divine community that contains diverse civilizations of plant and animal species. Better yet, think of it as a temple of the quality of a Chartres Cathedral or the like. There are beings here ancient in their evolution. They have been hardened by life and conditions of survival that we, as humans, cannot even imagine. Some, whom we call *pests,* appear more aggressive than others. Yet, as Tricia and I have discovered by observation, experimentation, and trial and error, most are simply living according to a Law of Nature unwritten or unspoken in human language. It is often our human fear or need for control that labels others as pests, enemies, or intruders, whereas, in truth, they are mere visitors, pilgrims, guests who find their place, measured by the time and cycle of seasons, then die or move on.

The fence that is our garden or yard's perimeter is really an illusion of our own human desire to control Nature by keeping things in and keeping things out. There is nothing wrong with this; it simply is what makes Nature that is a garden different from Nature that is wilderness. We should, however, want to approach each outdoor setting with the same intent: to create a boundless circle that shows compassionate celebration of the sacredness of all beings. But, even in this noble effort, there are always lessons to learn.

In a literal sense, here at Cortesia we have *had* to place a fence around our garden, although most of it is disguised in the woods or by buildings or shrubs. We have had to do this for only one reason: to keep deer out—to thwart the foraging tendencies of only *one* of God's creatures. We have numerous (and humorous) stories to tell about deer, and how they have occasionally breached the lines of defense. The fact is, from the perspective of many animals like deer, possum, raccoon, and the like, a garden is a heavenly grocery store with specialty items lined up by aisle: spinach and lettuce down Aisle A, strawberries down Aisle B, roses and dahlias down Aisle C, and so on. Our sensory abilities cannot even begin to shed any light on how mouthwatering our garden must appear and smell.

For some animals, a yard is a motel, giving them momentary asylum between journeys across the region. For still other animals—birds come to mind—a yard is a perfect place to fall in love, settle down, raise a family, and eat according to needs, before heading South for the winter. Some animals, like moles and voles, which are blind and never use the same underground tunnel twice, are merely following their instincts, sniffing out prime delicacies such as grubs and worms. A world-reknowned vermiculturist (worm expert) from India once conducted a workshop at Cortesia, and said that in India a mole is considered a goddess. This put a different light on matters in our garden. He also said that a healthy soil, with its strong immunity factors built into its tilth, was the best mole deterrent. If the redoubled effort we have put into our gardens' soils over the years is any indication, he is right—the moles have left.

My deepest compassion for the wildlife at Cortesia came by way of an experience that struck me at the quick of my soul. In the middle of the night, many years ago, I suddenly bolted out of a deep sleep realizing I had left the garden gate open. I ran stark naked out into the garden to find myself face to face with a foraging deer. Startled, she attempted to find a way out of the garden. She tried to leap the ten-foot-high fenceline, but was beaten back. Finally, I was able to chase her into a corner heavily secured by barbed-wire (which was removed after this incident). With one mighty heave, she attempted to jump through it, but one of her hind legs became viciously entangled and now she hung, almost suspended, by this one leg. I stepped carefully toward her until but a few feet away. And there I stood, naked and emotionally vulnerable, for the first time in my life gazing into the deep brown eyes of this truly stalwart creation. I could feel her fear, strength, courage, vulnerability, pride, and agony. And I was surprised to know that it felt no different than my own.

I talked to this deer gently, shivering in my own emotions. I attempted to survey her predicament, but she continued to alternately stuggle in vain and then pause in suspended silence. Then, it

Ten Suggestions for Creating a Reverent Habitat

· See everything in your refuge as part of a vast Web of Life, which you have volunteered to keep with love and respect.
· Practice reverence for the life of all creatures in your sanctuary and give this consciousness as a gift to the world.
· Watch, listen, and observe before taking action.
· Let curiosity prevail instead of fear or anxiety.
· Withhold judgement until well-informed.
· When in doubt, always err on the side of compassion.
· Create as natural a setting as possible, with a diversity of food and nectar-producing vegetation for each season.
· Know and learn about the wildlife common to your region and their needs for space, shelter, water, and food.
· Do not use poisons or toxic chemicals, for any reason!
· Always enter unconditionally with this question: "How can I serve thee?" Always visit with humility. Always leave with gratitude for blessings received.

happened, and this is what changed me: She began to bellow out in pain and anxiety. This voice haunts me to this day, for I know of few people who have ever heard a deer cry beyond snorting. This cry is of a spirit not unlike any other creature who knows that its freedom has been snatched from its soul. I prayed hard and fast to God to help this animal trapped in my own fenced creation. And then, suddenly, with one final effort, she broke loose and bolted for the freedom of the woods.

Sometimes we need a personal revelation to find our way back into God's dream of Creation. We can shorten the journey by desiring to withhold judgement about who or what is good or bad and to simply let curiosity, objective observation, or added knowledge help us create a welcome habitat. Sometimes we will learn that so-called pest infestations are cyclical by year, season, or climatical change; they may occur to balance out a predator–prey relationship, or point us toward a sign of deficiency in our soil or plants. We may also learn that the territorial range or habitat of larger animals has been so altered by humans through development, fencing, roads, and hunting, that they have become foragers of unfamiliar vegetation in even smaller unfamiliar settings such as a yard or garden. On the other hand, as we have found here at Cortesia, the foraging range of animals—deer, owls, even bees—may be more vast than we imagine, so an occasional visit is actually within the reasonable behavior of such a creature.

In short, as you consider ways to welcome and attract creatures to your backyard refuge, remember that your attitude, if based on fear, control, anxiety, and the like, may be the biggest deterrent. Most creatures are harmless, and serve a role in your setting, even if you don't know entirely what that may be. Although your place of refuge may only be a porch, patio, or balcony, by understanding some of the basic needs of birds, butterflies, squirrels, bugs, and the like, you can attract interesting and, almost always, *beneficial* critters. An outdoor sanctuary in which wildlife lives improves the aesthetic quality and liveability of that setting for you, your family, and friends, and may provide opportunities for outdoor education, photography, art, natural crafts, bird watching, animal husbandry, relaxation, and meditation, among many other activities. Perhaps the most important knowledge you need to create and maintain a natural habitat for wildlife is to provide for their basic needs.

THE FOUR NEEDS OF WILDLIFE

All creatures need space, shelter, water, and food. A small yard or garden can easily provide these essentials. However, you must learn to create a setting in which these needs can easily be met. Let me suggest that the best strategy is to create as natural a setting as possible with a diversity of food and nectar-producing vegetation for each season. By natural, I mean designing your refuge so that at least some part of it (even a *tiny* part) remains relatively untouched or more wild over the course of several seasons. By natural I also mean refraining from using chemical controls for weeds or bugs, synthetic fertilizers, and the like. And finally, by natural, I mean trying to grow vegetation native to your region and organically stewarding the soil it grows in. Such natives tend to be more disease and pest-resistant, drought-tolerant, and more hardy in severe weather.

Creating a natural habitat increases the diversity of insects, birds, and animals that visit. It is this very diversity that aids in keeping the overall balance among animal and insect populations. By focusing on space, shelter, water, and food, you will be doing your part to ensure that this bio-diversity thrives.

THE NEED FOR *Space*

The amount of space required by a particular species to meet its basic life needs, including breeding, is called its *home range* or *territory.* Territory generally increases with size of animal. Great horned owls, for example, each have a territory of many square miles, while a family of bluebirds requires only about one-half acre, and a raccoon may require a square mile or more. A bee may cruise as far as a mile or two for nectar, while a butterfly may find all its needs in its short lifetime within a couple acres or a few backyards. A little research at the library, or contacting an organiza-

tion, business, or individual versed in a particular animal species can provide you with more specific information about wildlife diversity in your area.

Nevertheless, "build or provide it, and they will come" is often true with a natural setting. Quite often, you will be amazed by how your little setting gets discovered or visited by certain wildlife. Case in point is the small pond and watercourse I built here at Cortesia. This is the only isolated source of water in over twenty acres, but within a couple of weeks after the pond's completion I was startled from a good night's sleep by the fierce croaking of several frogs. A year later, I had to do a few repairs to the pond. To my shock, as I moved a large stone near the waterline, a large newt appeared from behind. I have absolutely no idea where any of these visitors came from. They just appeared.

Nesting boxes are one of the easiest ways to attract wildlife such as birds, owls, or bats. For years, I merely let the diversity of our wooded and open meadow setting provide the backdrop or space for animals to inhabit. One day, while I was taking a nap at my desk, our friend Dan, a backyard bird specialist, stopped by and put up nine nesting boxes all around the garden as a gift. During that same week, Tricia and I purchased a one-of-a-kind birdhouse made from small stones, and mounted it on top of an eight-foot tall snag I left standing in the garden for just that purpose. Within a couple of weeks almost every box was occupied. More than that, I surrendered to the wonderful experience of birdwatching, and can finally now identify the many varieties that live and play here at Cortesia. The beauty of these boxes, as I quickly discovered, was that each one was occupied by a different species.

Certain vegetation can also attract select species, especially when it is used as a food source. Every yard or patio/balcony, for example, is a perfect space for hummingbirds and butterflies. Even a shallow saucer of water will attract a passing dragonfly or two. In lieu of a hummingbird feeder (the sugar-laden water is not healthy for hummingbirds), simply plant or display plants with red flowers (fuschias and impatiens for decks are common). Hummingbirds are ecstatic about red. The "butterfly bush" (Buddleia), with its intoxicating, long, purple-spiked flowers, also magnetically attracts dozens of butterflies to it for a feeding frenzy.

Remember, even a modicum of space is most likely large enough to attract certain wildlife to it. Provide shelter, water, and food sources in or near that space and your wildlife sanctuary will flourish.

THE NEED FOR *Shelter*

Good shelter or cover is essential for all wildlife and has three protective functions:

- **Hiding** *cover* as protection from predators.
- **Nesting** *cover* as protection of nesting sites.
- **Thermal** *cover* as protection from heat or cold.

Here are some useful suggestions for creating shelter for birds and other small wildlife in your refuge. Refer to the useful sidebars for specific names of vegetation mentioned.

The value of trees. Tree cavities (especially those of a standing dead tree, called a *snag*) are critical to a number of animals. They may serve as a den or nesting site for squirrels, raccoons, and birds, like woodpeckers and bluebirds. A tree's canopy and limb structure also provide perching

Common Food-Providing Trees

Deciduous	Conifers
Alder	Fir
Beech	Hemlock
Crabapple	Red cedar
Dogwood	Spruce
Oak	White pine
Willow	

and resting spots. Hawks, ravens, crows, and vultures all prefer the perching site of a limb or dead tree. All conifers (such as Eastern red cedar) offer important year-round shelter and windbreak. Sources of excellent food *and* cover are pines, evergreen oaks, southern magnolia, and trees that have a tendency toward hollowness, such as tupelos, sycamores, maples, and oaks.

The value of shrubs. Shrubs are perhaps more important than trees in providing for wildlife needs. They grow faster and supply food, cover, and nesting sites for wildlife that live near the ground. Variously sized shrubs and wild grasses (especially if unmowed until late spring or summer) will significantly increase the diversity of wildlife.

The value of ground cover and brush. These types of vegetation are critical in attracting wildlife. This habitat level provides the most diversity of shelter and food, and also provides the most basic backdrop for the predator–prey drama. Ground cover such as grasses, mosses, ferns, and wildflowers are perfect habitat for small animals such as box turtles, toads, mice, garden snakes, ground birds, and a host of insects. Ground holes provide homes for rabbits, skunks, opossums, and, of course field mice, groundhogs, gophers, moles, and voles, among other small creatures.

Other natural shelter for birds and small animals may be found in brush such as wild berries and wild hazelnuts, and in rockpiles and stone walls, decaying stumps and standing dead trees. One of our family's favorite viewpoints into the all-season life of birds is just outside the bathroom window. The wild blackberry bushes here provide wonderful shelter and food.

A very beneficial gesture in providing ground cover is to build or leave a brush pile made from

Common Fruit-Bearing Shrubs and Vines

Summer

Blackberry
Blueberry
Cherry
Currant
Gooseberry
Mulberry
Raspberry
Serviceberry

Fall

Bittersweet
Dogwood, redosier
Huckleberry, evergreen
Grape
Highbush cranberry
Juniper
Kiwi
Privet, Rosehips, Salal

Winter/Spring

Barberry
Cotoneaster
Mountain ash
Pyrancantha

Bayberry (wax myrtle)
Holly
Osoberry
Russian olive

general garden debris and limbs or twigs trimmed from trees and shrubs. You can leave this material in a remote corner, behind a wooden screen or taller shrub, or even piled over a stump or crossed logs. It never fails that when I casually walk by such a pile, no matter what season, I startle some ground bird like a junco or a foraging nuthatch. You can also provide additional shelter environments by keeping certain plants untrimmed, such as rose bushes, pyrancantha, wild hazelnuts, berry vines, and the lower limbs of evergreen trees like pine, spruce, and fir. Find a balance in your desire for order in your yard or garden and knowing that an element of disorder or natural roughness is the more natural attractor of wildlife.

The value of an edge effect. Ecologists call that setting where one type of dominant landscape intersects with another the *edge effect*. Here is where the greatest variety of wildlife can be found—where a brushy or grassy field or meadow adjoins the woods, where a garden adjoins a field, where plants or native vegetation grow around a pond or watercourse, where a wildflower or native-grass-planted bed adjoins denser foilage of trees, shrubs, or the more open area of a large lawn or meadow. At the edge of such settings, a large number of plants can thrive, providing in their variety a natural vegetative magnet for wildlife.

Here at Cortesia, the two acres of gardens surrounding our house is a virtual melting pot for flourishing varieties of vegetation and wildlife. This is because we are nestled right on the edge of deep woods and a large meadow, part of which is our lush vegetable, fruit, herb, and floral garden, and part of which is left wild to grow grasses and wildflowers (this is the unfenced area where the deer can forage to their heart's content). The interplay of many varieties of animals and insects on this edge provides a marvelous daily visual diet of live Nature for our family to watch.

To create more edge to your setting consider these options. Leave part of an open field uncut.

What, no open field? Then leave a rough, wilder growth around the boundaries of your yard or garden. Let grass grow taller between cuttings. Don't pick up all your fallen leaves. Let the area around a pond or watercourse grow more naturally (everybody thinks our pond is a natural spring simply because it *looks* so natural). Consider leaving a partially submerged log or rock in your pond, where it can be shelter for fish or an attachment or sunning site for aquatic insects, dragon-flies, and other small animals attracted to water. Plant a few more rocks in beds, creating sheltered crevices for spiders, beetles (two of the most absolutely beneficial insects to have around), and per-haps another creature or two (yes, unfortunately, slugs will take up housing there as well).

Providing shelter in your refuge is a way of saying to God's creatures "your well-being is my concern." You don't need to fear that you will be overrun by critters of all shapes and sizes. The fact is, you probably will be, but you won't know it. You see, a Law of Nature is diversity, and where there is diversity there are natural checks and balances between species that insure control. Of course, it is not a perfect world, and sometimes a predator will invade a space for certain reasons. Even then, however, such imbalance may be temporary, righting itself as new beneficial predators enter into the drama, certain diseased vegetation is removed, the soil is upgraded, or a change in climate or season provides the solution.

THE NEED FOR *Water*

Water, and the sound of water, is one of the most important attractors in a natural setting. Whereas the moisture from fruits and berries, rain, dew, and standing water such as puddles, melt-ing snow, and bogs are all vital sources for liquid nourishment (not to mention streams, creeks, springs, ponds, and lakes on larger acreage), it most often is the water *you* provide that will be cru-cial in attracting birds, butterflies, and other species to your sanctuary. For this reason, the creation of a small pond, watercourse, birdbath, and other water-holding objects, such as small bowls or a slightly hollowed-out rock is highly beneficial to wildlife.

Consider that if your sanctuary is providing nesting sites for birds, then a convenient water (and food) source is important for their comfort and survival. Parents often carry water in their beaks for their young, who eat as much as twice their weight each day. Most birds like shallow water for bathing (less than one inch for songbirds), so make sure that whatever water source you create has a shallow area. Hummingbirds find the water in birdbaths too deep to use, so place shal-low saucers of water near your red-flowered plants for them to bathe in.

Moving water is a keynote for wildlife, especially if it spills into still and shallow eddies. Birds love to bathe in such places. In a pond, it is important to have shallow areas. You can create a loaf-ing island, such as an exposed rock, or a crook created by a partially submerged log. A host of small creatures such as frogs, lizards, newts, turtles, and water-loving birds will frequent such natural environments. Similarly, sunning rocks near water sources do wonders for butterflies who often dip quickly in water, then land nearby to dry.

Birds will give your place of refuge a very comforting feeling, a real sense of wildlife sanctuary. Remember that birds, being cautious animals, will often perch near a water source before dropping down for a quick drink, a splash, and subsequent preening. For this reason, birdbaths and feeders should have about ten to twelve feet of open space on all sides for birds to view approaching predators (especially cats). These same birdbaths should also be cleaned and refilled with water regularly, even in winter, unless stored for safety.

Make sure you place a viewing bench or seat in a place where you can observe the activities of animals near water. You will receive unmatched hours and years of joy and wonder.

THE NEED FOR *Food*

Appropriate landscaping of any sanctuary intended to attract wildlife (especially birds) is key to providing food sources. With careful planning you can provide year-round food of four different types:

· Seeds and nuts
· Berries and soft fruits
· Insects
· Nectar-rich flowering plants

These foods are more easily provided by adopting these five simple strategies:

Strategy 1: Promote Diversity. As stated earlier, diversity is a biological law of Nature that is beneficial to both vegetal and animal/insect species. Provide as many different plant species as possible, especially easier-to-grow species native to your region, to fill the great diversity of wildlife needs for food and cover. If your setting is already very natural, you probably have a good variety of grasses, shrubs, flowers, and trees that don't require you to do much more. However, even in a small space such as a patio or balcony, where plants mostly exist in pots and planters, strive for varieties of plants and colors, perhaps a small tree, an ornamental grass, even a basin or barrel of water with submerged rocks. By creating a diverse grouping of vegetation and natural features you increase the likelihood of "being discovered."

Strategy 2: Plant for Structural Layering. Select plants that create as natural an effect as possible, vertically and horizontally. This should include wild native and ornamental grasses; low,

Supplemental Food for Some Common Birds

White Proso Millet

Brown-headed Cowbird
Dark-eyed Junco
House (English) Sparrow
Mourning Dove
Sparrows (most)
Red-winged Blackbird

Oil (Black) Sunflower

Cardinal
Chickadees
Evening Grosbeak
Purple & House Finch
Mourning Dove

Hulled Sunflower

American Goldfinch
Common Crackle
House Finch
White-throated Sparrow

Peanut Kernels

Blue Jay
Tufted Titmouse
Mourning Dove

Black-Striped Sunflower

Brown Thrasher
Chickadees
Common Grackle
Pine Siskin

Scrub Jay
Sparrows (some)
Tufted Titmouse
White & Red-breasted Nuthatch

medium, and tall shrubs and flowers; and varied sizes of trees. Trees, for example, make an excellent edge around a setting followed by taller shrubs and flowers in front of which grow lower plants and ground covers. Check the sidebar for a list of some deciduous and conifer food-providing trees.

Shrubs are excellent sources of food and cover. They also allow you to create screens and rooms in your favorite setting, among many other uses. Check the sidebar for common fruit-bearing shrubs and vines to consider in your sanctuary.

By structurally layering the vegetation in your setting you create visual–aesthetic interest that in its artistry, color, and natural lighting touches that sensual side of the soul. The bonus is that you have also enhanced the quality of habitat for wildlife.

Strategy 3: *Allow for Designated Wild Areas.* The creation of a so-called wild area in your sanctuary may seem antithical to your vision of an orderly, inspiring sanctuary and, really, the choice is always yours. But, a little natural sense of wildness can be *the* source of the greatest visitation and diversity of wildlife. To watch the comings and goings of animal and insect species over the seasons, as they interact with these fringes of wildness, may be a rewarding pasttime.

Visitors to Cortesia perhaps are most attracted to its feeling of naturalness. Nature's will is allowed to express itself freely within certain loosely prescribed boundaries. Our beds are not prissy, but neither are they chaotic. Sure, they may have rock or wood borders, but these are not so manicured that a blade of grass or a centipede would be paralyzed with fear to cross over. Herbs abound around the garden, even underfoot. A regionally respected herbalist loves to conduct classes here. Our woods are in what is called the herbal stage of development but, as she quickly points out to students, the very ground underfoot is a literal herbal pharmacy: prunella, dandelion, white clover, violet, plantain, English daisy, and so on. Students often make salves from the herbs growing throughout the garden.

By the same token, we let a bit of wildness creep into our vegetable beds—volunteers of feverfew, calendula, rosemary, greens, celery, fennel, amaranth, yarrow, mint, Russian kale, among many others. This diversity does wonders for insect management, and provides great color and textural variety. Added to this wildness is also our decision to let numerous plants and crops go through their whole life cycle. Wintering over kale that has gone to seed, for example, often provides the first blossoming flowers (beautiful yellow) in the spring garden, getting a jump even on the fruit trees. This gesture is loved by very early arriving bees who wait for weeks until the trees are in full bloom to pollinate.

If you haven't tried it, take the risk. Don't worry about what your neighbors or family members think. Let go of that embedded message to always be in control of the garden. Go a little wild. Critters will love you for it.

Strategy 4: *Provide Seasonal Food Sources.* Take into consideration the migratory and hibernation patterns of certain species and the winter habits of others. Providing seasonal food sources will meet the needs of area wildlife year round. Remember, different species need a variety of seeds and nuts, berries and soft fruits, insects, and nectar-rich flowering plants.

Annual flowers, such as asters, daisies, sunflowers, marigolds, and herbs provide late summer seeds for species who need fall and winter seed sources for protein. Berries provide excellent summer and fall soft fruit. Wild blackberries are an important keynote plant species for many small animals, as are pyrancantha, wild grape, wild rose, greenbrier, bittersweet, huckleberry, salal, and elderberry, among others.

Providing supplemental food for birds, especially in winter, can greatly increase the number

HOW TO WIN A BUTTERFLY'S HEART ♥ ♥

and species of birds that visit your sanctuary. A crabapple tree is an important winter food source for birds and squirrels. Bird feeders are perhaps the most common way to provide food, but remember that some birds are ground feeders. Many excellent books and resources are available to help you. Check out the sidebar listing favorite birds seeds of common birds. When feeding birds, always remember to have their safety in mind, so hang feeders where there is at least a ten to twelve foot clearing around them for safe entrance and exit, and make sure the food remains dry.

If you love butterflies, then you can do a few special things to attract such wonderfully benign species to your sanctuary. Butterflies need a healthy mix of flowering annuals, perennials, and shrubs that will provide nectar and egg-laying sites for the adults. Once the eggs hatch, the larva (caterpillars) have voracious and selective appetites (don't worry, they have very little effect on the overall plant life in your garden). After three to six weeks the pupal stage is entered and, after one to two weeks they emerge as adult butterflies, their metamorphosis complete. Adult and larval food plants are your best assurance of a long-term supply of butterfly visitors. Read the sidebars for a partial list of nectar plants for butterflies and bees and native plants for butterfly larva.

Strategy 5: Avoid All Pesticide Use. Perhaps the greatest risk to wildlife today, besides shrinking diverse habitat, is poisoning. Although the reverent intent to provide a safe haven for Nature and wildlife would seem to preclude any use of pesticides, fungicides, herbicides, and synthetic fertilizers, I feel compelled to caution those of you who might believe that some form of human intervention using these inputs *is* necessary to create an orderly, well-maintained setting. The truth is exactly the opposite. At the very least, the price of such an approach may be a somewhat antiseptic sanctuary environment.

The greatest abusers of synthetic inputs are not farmers but backyard gardeners and homeowners where the attitude that "more is better" often means more intense application than recom-

Some Common Nectar Plants for Butterflies and Bees

Annuals

Amaranth	Aster	Cornflower
Cosmos	Dahlia	Heliotrope
Lantana	Marigold	Nicotiana
Petunia	Sage	Strawflower
Sunflower	Tithonia	Zinnia

Note: Removing dead blossoms will increase new blooms and maximize nectar.

Perennials

Bee Balm	Butterfly weed	Chives
Coral Bells	Coreopsis	Cranesbill
Echinacea	Geranium	Daisy
Daylily	Goldenrod	Joe-pye weed
Lavender	Liatris	Lythrum
Mints	Phlox	Rosemary
Rubideckia	Sedums	Violet

Note: Allowing seed pods to remain in fall will provide bird food during winter.

Shrubs

Abelia, Butterfly bush (Buddleia), honeysuckle, mock-orange, privet, spice bush

NATIVE PLANTS FOR BUTTERFLY LARVA

Goldenrod	Milkweed	Nettle
Thistle	Tick Trefoil	Queen Anne's Lace
Wild grasses	Herbs	

Note: Creating a hedgerow of these wild plants will make a perfect home for butterfly larvae and other beneficial insects.

mended. The fact is, most backyard gardeners have in their shed or garage enough garden- or yard-related chemicals or poisons to kill every citizen in a small community. In Nature, such poisons create harmful levels of residues in the soil, plants, fruits, water table, and even in pets, children, and adults. (I recently learned that a common poisonous residue found on home carpets and floors is brought in on shoes and feet which have walked or played on lawns sprayed and fertilized to control weeds or promote growth.) Additionally, these poisons directly combat Nature's attempt to promote diversity and balance among species. Even organic inputs, such as botanicals, have a level of toxicity that plays havoc with the balance of insect life. In both instances, for example, a compound used to control a specific insect or condition usually has a detrimental effect on other beneficial species within the predator–prey web.

Please, educate yourself about how to co-create with Nature. It may take some time and trial and error, and you may have to adjust your expectations or preconceived notions about working (and playing) with Nature. However, your conscience will be well rewarded. Don't aspire to be like the old gentleman in the story at the beginning of this chapter. Don't be the scarecrow in your sanctuary. Be its devoted Keeper. There are many little gods and goddesses there worthy of your heart's kindness and love.

For the moment, let's return to a symbol of unity shared at the beginning of this book: the *hearth.* When you plan for the well-being of God's many creatures who may visit your place of refuge, you are in a sense offering them a hearth, a place for communion, community *and* common-unity. You offer them your part of the *Earth.* You offer them your *heart.* You offer them a compassionate *ear* in which to *hear* and sense their needs. Lastly, you offer them the *art* of your creativity and sensitivity with Nature in order to meet their needs for space, shelter, water, and food. Such charity, as a Cortesian way of life, is not without its setbacks or disappointments, but reverence is taught and gained through many lessons and teachers. By entering our place of refuge with the unconditionality of this simple question—"How can I serve Thee?"—we become philanthropists for Creation in our own backyards. Such purity of intention does not go unnoticed within the Web of Life. When the first butterfly lands in the palm of your hand, you will feel touched by the spirit of St. Francis. Your setting will feel holy and blessed. You too will feel like a hummingbird sipping of peace.

The Indian sage, Eknath Easwaran writes in his inspiring book, *The Compassionate Universe:* "We need people with the artistry to live in simplicity as the hummingbird does, enjoying the nectar without bruising the fruit." Truly enjoy the nectar of Creation in your sanctuary without bruising Nature. Then, you will extend your compassion in knowing that this whole planet, with all Her many species, is a divine haven worth keeping with reverence. At this point, you will become a Keeper of the Earth Sanctuary. Blessed be!

TIPS FOR BUTTERFLY LOVERS

· Butterflies are unable to fly if their body temperature is too low. That is why they like sunbathing—it warms up their wings for flight. Lay out some nice flat rocks here and there for them to rest on.

· Since butterfly larvae may only feed on the leaves of one or two plants in your garden, once you see what they prefer you may want to plant extra, so there is enough for all of you. But the more native plants you have (wild ones even more so than cultivated varieties!) the happier those larvae will be.

· Butterflies also enjoy water, so place a few shallow trays or saucers of water on the ground.

· Grouping several of a certain type of nectar-rich plant together makes it easier for the butterflies to feed.

· Think of your setting as a habitat that provides plenty of food for everyone. In that spirit, occasional damage to plants will not seem offensive, but natural!

The Gift of Sanctuary:

THE CORTESIA SANCTUARY PROJECT

Perhaps the most sacred task in your life is to open fully to your Spirit, that you may find and use your unique gifts for the benefit of all. Indeed, it can be said that this sense of Spirit resides in the sanctuary of your soul—as a compassionate inner light fully capable, in its radiance, to spread the warmth and beauty of love, reverence, and gratitude wherever you go.

We believe that the quest for sanctuary should be a daily one. In an unpredicatable world, we need more constants, more spiritual *and* safe reference points. The commitment to find daily refuge, in order to revitalize and sustain our spirit, takes effort and devotion. Knowing the great amount of conscious effort our own family has taken to live with reverence for life, we believe others might like to share in our gift of sanctuary.

We founded The Cortesia Sanctuary Project, a nonprofit educational organization, in 1995 to do just that. The Project's mission is to inspire, educate, and assist people worldwide to develop a sense of sanctuary in their lives as a means to increase personal well-being, foster respect for cultural and biological diversity, and demonstrate gratitude and reverence for the Earth and all its species and natural environments.

A central element of the Project is to help people empower their lives through embracing

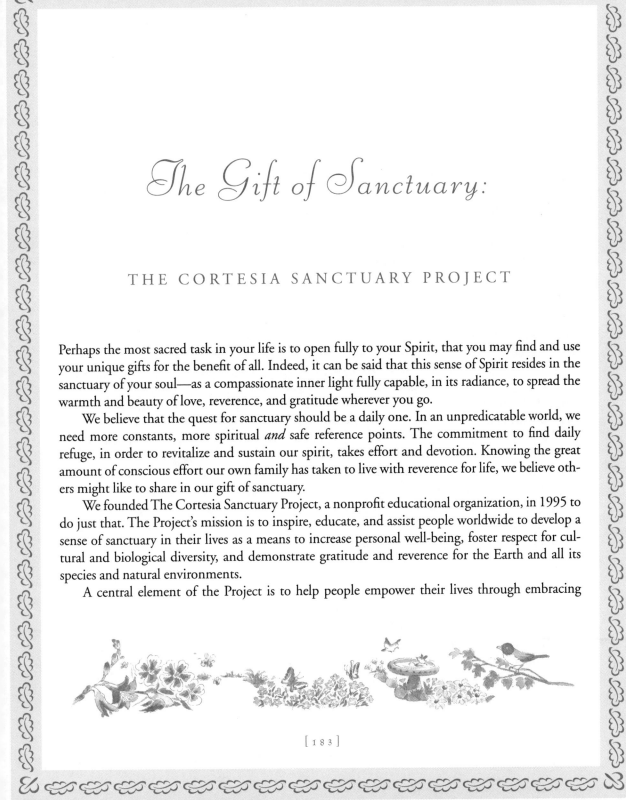

what we call "The Seven Principles of Sanctuary Work." These life-guiding principles ask the individual to find a balance between a life-enhancing philosophy and reverential practice of that philosophy in daily life. The Seven Principles of Sanctuary Work include:

    I.   Embrace your sacredness.
   II.   Embrace the sacredness of the world.
  III.   Acknowledge the value of sanctuary for yourself, Nature, and all other beings and places.
  IV.   Create sacred time and space for yourself every day.
   V.   Practice reverence for life.
  VI.   Practice nonjudgement and compassion.
 VII.   Give of yourself to bring more joy, beauty, hope and peace into the world.

Perhaps these Principles sound a little familiar to you. They should, for we have embedded them throughout our discussion in this book of the seven design elements of a Sanctuary Garden. Now we offer you the gift of sanctuary in your life—for your home, a room, and, yes, for your yard or garden. Many hundreds of people throughout the world have voluntarily registered their setting as a sanctuary through the Cortesia Sanctuary Project. These range from large acreage to intimate outdoor settings, from buildings to bedrooms for the seriously ill or dying, from a gift to oneself or family to a gift for a friend or neighbor. In every instance, people are motivated to demonstrate that both life and place are worthy of the pursuit of peace of mind, soul, and spirit.

Each participant receives a numbered certificate of registration of their setting, a thirty-two page handbook, educational brochures, and one entry into the Project's worldwide database of sanctuaries. They also receive a sanctuary sign of choice to display at their setting (one is designed for outdoor settings, the other for indoors). Minimum suggested donation to cover costs and mailing is twelve to fifteen dollars in U.S. funds.

For a Project registration brochure, please send a self-addressed envelope with fifty-five cents in U.S. postage, or equivalent to:

The Cortesia Sanctuary Project
84540 McBeth Rd.
Eugene, OR, U.S.A. 97405
(541) 343-9544

You may also visit our website on the internet, complete with numerous articles, tip sheets and registration information. You may also find product and ordering information for our line of twenty-three *Cortesia Flower Essence Blends*. Our website is located at:

http://www.cortesia.org
You may e-mail the Project at: cortesia@cortesia.org or
sanctuary@cortesia.org

We are very interested in how people have created sanctuary in their lives. And, of course, we are interested in hearing about how you have created your own unique Sanctuary Garden. (Know of a splendid example of a Sanctuary Garden? Tell us about that, too.) Please write us about your efforts, and send a photo or two if you like. However, if you want to make a pilgrimage to Cortesia to visit our gardens, please give us plenty of notice. We love appreciative visitors, but also feel compelled to balance our public life with our own need for sanctuary. We are sure you understand exactly what we mean. Peace be with you. Forrest, Tricia, and Sonji McDowell.

The Gift of Sanctuary

Suggested Readings

Ackerman, Diane. *A Natural History of the Senses.* New York: Vintage Books, 1991.

Alexander, Christopher. *A Pattern Language.* New York: Oxford University Press, 1977.

Anderson, Lorraine (ed.). *Sisters of the Earth.* New York: Vintage Books, 1991.

Anderson, William and Clive Hicks. *Green Man.* San Francisco: HarperCollins, 1990.

Barnes, Emilie. *Time Began in a Garden.* Eugene, OR: Harvest House Publishers, 1995.

Bell, Graham. *The Permaculture Garden.* London: Thorsons, 1994.

Berry, Thomas. *The Dream of the Earth.* San Francisco: Sierra Club Books, 1988.

Bly, Robert. *The Kabir Book.* Boston: Beacon Press, 1977.

Cox, Jeff. *Landscaping with Nature.* Emmaus, PA: Rodale Press, 1991.

Dennis, J.V. *The Wildlife Gardener.* New York: Alfred A. Knopf, Inc., 1985.

Druse, Ken. *The Natural Garden.* New York: Clarkson N. Potter, 1989.

Easwaran, Eknath. *The Compassionate Universe.* Petaluma, CA: Nilgiri Press, 1989.

Greenlee, John. *The Encyclopedia of Ornamental Grasses.* Emmaus, PA: Rodale Press, 1992.

Handelsman, Judith. *Growing Myself.* New York: Plume, 1997.

Hanh, Thich Nhat. *Touching Peace.* Berkeley, CA: Parallax Press, 1992.

Harper, Peter. *The Natural Garden Book.* New York: Simon & Schuster Inc., 1994.

Herwig, Modeste. *Colorful Gardens.* New York: Sterling Publishing Co., 1994.

Hesse, Hermann. *Wandering.* New York: Farrar, Straus & Giroux, 1972.

Holmes, Roger (ed.). *Taylor's Guide to Natural Gardening.* New York: Houghton Mifflin Co., 1993.

Kress, Stephen W. *The Audubon Society Guide to Attracting Birds.* New York: Scribner's, 1985.

London, Peter. *No More Second Hand Art.* Boston: Shambhala, 1989.

Martin, Laura C. *The Wildflower Meadow Book: A Gardener's Guide.* Chester, Conn.: Globe Pequot Press, 1990.

Matott, Justin. *My Garden Visits.* New York: Ballantine Books, 1996.

Suggested Readings

Moore, Thomas. *Care of the Soul.* New York: HarperCollins, 1992.

Moore, Thomas. *The Re-enchantment of Everyday Life.* New York: HarperCollins, 1996.

Osler, Mirabel. *The Garden Bench.* New York: Simon & Schuster, 1991.

Paul, Anthony and Yvonne Rees. *The Water Garden.* New York: Viking Penguin, 1986.

Schweitzer, Albert. *Reverence for Life.* New York: The Pilgrim Press, 1969.

Sedenko, Jerry. *The Butterfly Garden: Creating Beautiful Gardens to Attract Butterflies.* New York: Villard Books, 1991.

Skolimowski, Henryk. *A Sacred Place to Dwell.* Rockport, MA: Element Inc., 1993.

Stein, Sara. *Noah's Garden.* New York: Houghton Mifflin Co., 1993.

Swan, James A. *Sacred Places.* Sante Fe, NM: Bear & Company, Inc., 1990.

Swindells, Philip. *The Overlook Water Gardener's Handbook.* New York: The Overlook Press, 1984.